CREDIT SECRETS BIBLE

5 IN 1

REVEALING THE PATH TO FINANCIAL FREEDOM WITH
AN 800+ FICO SCORE | YOUR GUIDE TO UNLOCKING
CREDIT SECRETS FOR PROSPERITY

ALEC ROWE

TABLE OF CONTENTS

BOOK THREE
CREDIT MANAGEMENT AND DEBT REDUCTION

BOOK FOUR
PROTECTING YOUR CREDIT

BOOK FIVE
LONG-TERM FINANCIAL PLANNING

INTRODUCTION

"Credit Secrets Bible 5 in 1," is your ultimate guide to mastering your credit, repairing damaged credit scores, safeguarding your financial identity, and building long-term wealth for you and your family. This comprehensive book contains five individual books that work together to provide you with a roadmap toward financial freedom.

In Book 1: Understanding Credit Basics, we lay down foundations for credit literacy by discussing the importance of credit, how credit scores and various types of accounts function, and tackle common myths about credit. We also explore the essential factors contributing to a strong credit score and teach you how to obtain, understand, and improve your credit reports.

Book 2: Credit Repair Strategies takes you through a step-by-step process that involves assessing your current credit situation, devising practical goals to improve it, employing do-it-yourself techniques for disputing inaccuracies or negotiating with creditors, and determining when to consider professional help like credit repair companies or counselors.

As we move to Book 3: Credit Management and Debt Reduction, we help you develop a credit-friendly budget that empowers you to manage expenses effectively, as well as forging smart strategies for managing your credit cards and reducing debt using different consolidation options without falling prey to common traps.

Book 4: Protecting Your Credit focuses on securing your hard-earned position from identity theft threats and fraud risks. We also introduce the powerful 609 Letter Template for Credit Repair - an advanced strategy used by many people successfully to purge negative items from their reports. And lastly, we share other alternative strategies along with legal considerations and resources exclusive to our readers.

Finally, in Book 5: Long-Term Financial Planning, we guide you on creating long-lasting wealth by setting milestones, tracking progress throughout your investment journey while adjusting your financial plans accordingly. Insights into achieving financial independence are shared so that you can create lasting legacies for future generations.

As you embark on this transformative journey through the *"Credit Secrets Bible 5 in 1,"* rest assured that you are arming yourself with the knowledge and tools needed to create a personalized credit action plan and ultimately chart a path towards lasting financial prosperity.

BOOK ONE

UNDERSTANDING CREDIT BASICS

INTRODUCTION

In this first book of the CREDIT SECRETS BIBLE 5 in 1 series, you will learn the essentials of credit and how it impacts your financial life. From understanding credit scores to debunking common myths, this book will help you lay a strong foundation for building and maintaining a healthy credit history. Additionally, you will be guided on how to obtain your credit report and gain insights into improving your credit score.

CHAPTER 1
INTRODUCTION TO CREDIT

CREDIT ALLOWS INDIVIDUALS AND BUSINESSES ACCESS TO FUNDS, PRODUCTS OR SERVICES, WITH THE understanding that the borrowed amount will be repaid at a later date. In essence, credit is a trust-based system where one party expresses confidence in another's ability to repay debt. This introduction to credit will explore the concept, types of credit, essential features, and consequences related to the improper use of credit.

At the heart of the credit system lies the idea of borrowing – an individual or business receives money or asset based on trust in their ability to return it within agreed-upon terms. Credit enables consumers to make important purchases without having immediate access to funds, such as buying a house, paying for education, or starting a business venture. It can also help individuals manage their cash flow by providing temporary financial relief in emergencies.

There are several types of credit available in the financial market. The two primary categories are 'revolving credit' and 'installment credit.' Revolving credit allows for multiple uses and flexible repayment terms. Examples include credit cards or a line of credit provided by a bank. Meanwhile, installment credit involves borrowing a specific amount of money that is repaid over time through regular payments until it reaches zero balance. Common examples are auto loans, mortgages, and student loans.

Credit scores are an essential aspect of the credit system. They provide a numeric representation of an individual's or business' reliability and soundness for assuming debt based on historical data. The most common scoring mechanism is Fair Isaac Corporation (FICO) scoring ranging from 300 (poor) to 850 (excellent). A higher score denotes greater trustworthiness and lower lending risk for creditors.

Interest rates also play an essential role in understanding how credit works. When borrowing money, interest rates represent the cost associated with using the borrowed funds. The interest rate on a loan or a credit card is determined by several factors, including the borrower's credit score, the length of the loan, and market conditions. In general, higher credit scores lead to lower interest rates, while individuals with lower scores may face higher interest rates due to increased risk perception.

While credit has many benefits, it also comes with potential pitfalls. Misuse or mismanagement of credit can result in negative consequences such as damaged credit scores, higher interest rates on future loans and inability to access critical loans like mortgages when needed. Moreover, excessive use of credit without proper financial planning may lead to unmanageable debt and financial distress.

To prevent such consequences, responsible use of credit is essential. It includes timely payments of bills and debts, keeping an eye on one's credit utilization ratio by monitoring balances on one's revolving accounts, and maintaining a diverse mix of different types of credits.

THE IMPORTANCE OF CREDIT

At an individual level, credit provides opportunities and access to resources that are essential to economic success. With sound credit practices, people can secure loans to finance significant purchases like homes or vehicles and obtain lines of credit to fund education and future business ventures. The importance of establishing and maintaining a good credit score cannot be overstated. A strong credit rating opens doors for individuals to lead better lives by enabling them to be deemed trustworthy borrowers by potential lenders.

Furthermore, creditworthiness also impacts employment opportunities for some professionals as employers evaluate financial stability as a marker for overall responsibility. Essentially, a solid credit history reflects an individual's ability to manage their finances prudently, which may translate into better job prospects and increased earning potential.

Another critical aspect of credit is its ability to help people navigate unforeseen challenges that may surface in their lives, such as sudden illness or unforeseen expenses. Accessible lines of credit provide flexibility and security during hardships or emergencies, granting individuals the financial cushion they might need during trying times.

At a global level, the concept of credit stimulates economic growth by facilitating transactions among nations and businesses. The flow of capital enabled by lines of credit can often serve as catalysts for the development of new markets, promoting job creation across borders. Moreover, the ease in obtaining financing encourages entrepreneurship and innovation across various industries.

Investments made with borrowed funds – be it in large-scale projects like infrastructure developments or support for small businesses – foster economic progress worldwide. Credit allows countries to invest in themselves while fostering sustainable development with eventual debt repayment integrated into the financial plan.

The impact of credit extends beyond merely stimulating the economy; it enables governments to shape fiscal policies and address the needs of their populace. Public funds may be raised through the issuance of government bonds, generating long-term capital that can be used to finance schools, hospitals, and other essential amenities. Through carefully managed credit usage, governments can improve living standards for their citizens and pave the way for future opportunities.

However, it is crucial to recognize that the benefits of credit should be weighed against the potential risks. Mismanaged credit can lead to overwhelming debt, both at individual and national levels. Global financial crises and personal bankruptcies can result from unsustainable borrowing practices. An awareness of proper credit management and responsible borrowing practices are essential in order for individuals, businesses, and governments to reap the full benefits.

HOW CREDIT SCORES WORK

A credit score is a numerical representation of an individual's creditworthiness, which is used by financial institutions and lenders to evaluate the risk associated with providing credit to a borrower. The score gives lenders an idea of how likely a borrower is to repay their debts on time, and whether they are at a high or low risk of defaulting on a loan. Understanding how credit scores work is crucial to managing one's personal finances and can greatly affect one's ability to obtain credit for large purchases such as houses, cars, or investments.

Credit scores range from 300 to 850, and typically fall into five categories: poor (300-579), fair (580-669), good (670-739), very good (740-799), and excellent (800-850). A higher credit score indicates a lower risk for the lender as it suggests that the borrower has been responsible in managing their debt repayments in the past.

Several factors influence an individual's credit score. These factors include payment history, amount of debt owed, age of credit history, types of credit accounts, and recent applications for new credit lines or loans. Each of these factors plays a role in determining one's overall score.

1. Payment history: This factor comprises 35% of an individual's total credit score. Timely payments demonstrate financial responsibility and play a significant role in maintaining a healthy credit score. Late payments, defaults, or bankruptcy filings can negatively impact one's score.

2. Amount of debt owed: The total amount owed—also called the "credit utilization rate"—constitutes 30% of an individual's credit score. This figure is calculated by dividing the total debt reported by all available revolving lines of credit by the total available credit limit. A lower utilization ratio implies better financial management and will positively influence the overall score.

3. Age of credit history: The length of time that borrowers have maintained credit accounts can affect their credit scores. Longer and well-managed credit histories contribute to a higher rating and account for 15% of the total score.

4. Types of credit accounts: Having a mix of diverse credit accounts showcases the ability to manage various types of loans. Examples include mortgages, auto loans, credit cards, and personal loans. This factor carries a 10% weight in determining one's score.

5. Recent applications for new credit: Applying for multiple new loans or lines of credit in a short time can indicate increased risk. Lenders may perceive that the individual is facing financial difficulties or is unable to manage existing debts. This factor also accounts for 10% of an individual's total credit score.

In addition to determining borrowing eligibility, an individual's credit score also affects interest rates on loans and premiums on insurance policies. Higher scores generally result in more favorable terms and lower interest rates, which can save borrowers a significant amount of money in the long run.

To improve and maintain a healthy credit score, individuals should make an effort to pay their bills on time, avoid maxing out their available lines of credit, limit their requests for new loans or credit lines, and monitor their credit report for errors or signs of fraud.

COMMON CREDIT MYTHS

Credit scores, credit reports, and credit-related decisions have a significant impact on an individual's financial life. Many misconceptions and myths surround this topic; this article strives to debunk those myths and provide accurate information regarding credit.

Myth 1: Checking your own credit score frequently lowers it.

Reality: This is false. When individuals check their own credit score, it is considered a "soft inquiry," which does not lower the score. "Hard inquiries," such as applying for new loans or credit cards, might negatively impact the credit score. However, regularly checking your credit score and monitoring changes is a responsible financial habit.

Myth 2: You only have one credit score.

Reality: People have multiple credit scores based on different calculations. The most well-known scores are FICO and VantageScore, each with variations under different circumstances. Moreover, each of the three main credit bureaus—Experian, Equifax, and TransUnion—may report slightly different information based on the data they have access to.

Myth 3: Closing unused accounts will improve your credit score.

Reality: Closing unused accounts may decrease your available total credit limit, leading to a higher utilization ratio. A high utilization ratio may negatively affect your credit score. Keeping an older account open shows a longer payment history and positively impacts your overall score.

Myth 4: Income affects your credit score.

Reality: Contrary to popular belief, income does not directly impact your FICO or Vantage-Score ratings. While income may be considered in calculating an individual's ability to repay debts when applying for new loans or rental properties, it does not factor into their actual credit-worthiness.

Myth 5: Co-signing on a loan won't affect your own credit.

Reality: Co-signing on a loan means that you share equal responsibility for repayment with the primary borrower. If payments are missed or late, both parties' credit scores will be negatively impacted. Furthermore, if the primary borrower defaults on the loan, the co-signer will also be responsible for fulfilling the debt.

Myth 6: Paying off debt erases negative marks on credit reports.

Reality: While paying off debt is always a good idea, it won't automatically remove negative marks from your credit report. Collections accounts and late payments can remain on your report for up to seven years. Nevertheless, the negative impact of these marks lessens over time.

Myth 7: A weak credit history is better than no history at all.

Reality: A weak or damaged credit history may cause more harm than not having any history at all. Lenders often prefer extending loans to borrowers with thin or non-existent credit files, rather than those with negative histories. For individuals with no credit history, smart financial decisions and occasional use of secured financial products like secured credit cards help them build positive credit profiles over time.

Myth 8: All debt affects your credit score equally.

Reality: Different types of debt have varying impacts on credit scores. Revolving debts (such as credit card balances) carry more influence on lowering scores due to high utilization ratios compared to installment loans (such as mortgages or auto loans).

CHAPTER 2
BUILDING A STRONG CREDIT FOUNDATION

A STRONG CREDIT SCORE NOT ONLY ALLOWS YOU TO OBTAIN LOANS AND CREDIT CARDS WITH LOWER interest rates but is also pivotal in acquiring new employment opportunities, leasing homes or apartments, and handling everyday expenses. To construct a sturdy credit foundation, the first step involves understanding your current financial situation and credit score. Begin by analyzing your credit report obtained from trusted sources such as Experian, TransUnion, or Equifax. Carefully comb through each item on the report, ensuring its accuracy while identifying areas for improvement in your overall credit history.

ESTABLISHING CREDIT HISTORY

Building a solid credit history is like laying the cornerstone for your financial fortress. By establishing a strong credit foundation, you open doors to new opportunities, more lucrative borrowing options, and improved financial flexibility.

So, what exactly is credit history? It's a record of how well you've managed your debt obligations over time. This not only includes credit cards but also personal loans, mortgages, and other debts. Potential lenders and creditors analyze your credit history when they're deciding whether to grant or deny you credit. Having an excellent credit history means that you're seen as a responsible borrower in the eyes of these entities; hence, they're more likely to approve your credit applications. This section will guide you through the necessary steps to establish and improve your credit history.

1. Understand Your Credit Reports: The first step towards establishing credit history is understanding what makes up a credit report. Major credit bureaus like Equifax, Experian, and TransUnion collect information on your financial activities and compile them into a report that includes data such as credit accounts, payment history, credit utilization ratio, length of credit history, and recent inquiries.

2. Acquire A Secured Credit Card: For those who are just starting out and do not have an established credit history, obtaining a secured credit card can be an excellent way to begin building good credit history. These cards require a small deposit as collateral, usually equivalent to the card's limit. Regularly using this card for purchases and paying off the balance responsibly will contribute positively to your credit report.

3. Find A Co-Signer: Getting someone with good credit to co-sign on a loan or rental application can help you establish your initial credit history with less risk for potential lenders or landlords. As a co-signer takes responsibility if you fail to make payments, it is crucial that both parties understand the implications and risks before agreeing.

4. Become an Authorized User: Requesting a family member or close friend with good credit to add you as an authorized user on their account is another effective way of building your credit history without applying for new accounts independently. Ensure that the primary account holder pays the balance in full each month so that positive information is reported to your own credit report.

5. Apply for Credit Builder Loans: Credit builder loans are designed specifically for individuals looking to establish or improve their credit history. The borrowed amount is held in a separate account until the loan is paid off. Once all payments have been made on time, the borrower gains access to the funds and can benefit from the positive credit history generated by making timely payments.

6. Keep Your Credit Utilization Low: Having outstanding debts can negatively impact your credit history, especially if you have high balances on your accounts. Keep your credit utilization ratio – the percentage of available credit used – ideally below 30%. Having low balances demonstrates responsible credit management and improves your overall credit score.

7. Check Your Credit Report Regularly: Regularly checking your credit report allows you to catch any discrepancies or errors that could be affecting your creditworthiness. Dispute any inaccuracies immediately with the relevant credit bureaus and rectify any issues that may suggest fraudulent activity.

8. Pay Your Bills Timely: Paying bills on time plays a significant role in building a strong credit history. These include student loans, rent, utilities, and other financial obligations that may report missed payments to credit bureaus.

TYPES OF CREDIT ACCOUNTS

A credit account is a financial agreement where a lender extends funds to a borrower, who is trusted to repay it at a later date—usually with interest. The primary purpose of a credit account is to establish trust between creditors and borrowers. As you exhibit responsible borrowing habits over time, your credit score will improve, making it easier for you to qualify for various types of loans.

Understanding the different types of credit accounts is essential for managing your finances and building a strong credit history. As you continue reading, remember that credit accounts play a major role in determining your credit score, which in turn affects your ability to secure loans, mortgages, and other forms of financing.

Now that we have established what a credit account involves let's delve into some different types:

1. Revolving Credit Accounts: Revolving credit accounts are perhaps the most well-known type of credit available. As the name suggests, these accounts allow for an ongoing balance that can be paid off in full at any time or carried over from month to month. The most common form of revolving credit is the credit card. Within revolving credit accounts, there are two main subcategories:

1. *Unsecured:* These are typical credit cards that do not require any collateral. Issuers determine your eligibility based on factors like your income and existing indebtedness.
2. *Secured:* Secured cards require a security deposit that acts as collateral for the card issuer. These cards are designed for individuals with little or no credit history or those looking to improve their existing score.

2. Installment Credit Accounts: Installment credits are loans where you borrow a specific amount of money and agree to repay it with interest over a predetermined period. Examples include auto loans, mortgages, student loans, and personal loans.

Each installment loan has unique terms and conditions, such as the length of repayment, interest rate options (fixed or variable), and potential penalties for early repayment.

3. Open Credit Accounts: Also known as charge accounts, open credit accounts have no preset limit, but you must pay the balance in full each billing cycle. Failure to do so can result in steep fees and penalties. The most common example of an open credit account is the American Express Card; its iconic Green, Gold, and Platinum charge cards all fall under this category.

4. Retail Credit Accounts: Retail credit accounts are a subset of revolving credit accounts exclusively used for purchasing goods or services from a specific company. Department store cards and gas station cards are classic examples of retail credit accounts. These accounts typically come with high-interest rates and limited use cases.

5. Service Credit Accounts: Service credit accounts, such as utility accounts for electricity or water, can also play a role in your overall credit history. Timely payment of these bills reflects positively on your payment history.

By understanding these various types of credit accounts, you can make informed decisions about which one is best suited for your financial needs. Managing your accounts responsibly will not only help you maintain a healthy credit score but also establish long-term trust with creditors.

CREDIT SCORE FACTORS

Your credit score, a three-digit number that speaks volumes about your financial credibility, is like a mirror reflecting your financial habits. The moment you apply for credit, this number follows you like a shadow, influencing the outcome of every loan or credit decision made by potential lenders.

To fully grasp the power this numeric representation holds over your fiscal endeavors, it's essential to understand the factors that contribute to its calculation. Grab a comfy chair and settle in as we explore these five critical elements.

1. Payment History (35%): Your payment history is the single most influential factor in determining your credit score. Lenders are keen to know if you can meet your financial obligations consistently and on time. Late payments, defaults, and bankruptcies are red flags that could send your score plummeting.

Always make it a priority to pay your bills on time – even if it means setting-up auto-payments or creating calendar reminders. Should you falter here and there, don't beat yourself up too much; just make sure to get back on track as quickly as possible.

2. Credit Utilization (30%): The second most important factor affecting your credit score is credit utilization – essentially the ratio of your outstanding debt to available credit limits. Maxing out your cards may lead lenders to believe that you're in financial distress, resulting in a dip in your overall rating.

A good rule of thumb is to maintain a utilization rate lower than 30% across all accounts. To achieve this, consider requesting a higher limit from your credit provider or spreading charges among multiple cards.

3. Length of Credit History (15%): Think back to when you first started exploring the realm of finance and opened that initial credit account — was it an innocent student loan or perhaps that very first credit card? These milestones add up to your length of credit history, and the longer this span, the better it looks to potential lenders.

Predictability and stability are vital in establishing good credit, so it's wise to avoid closing old accounts unless necessary or opening too many accounts simultaneously.

4. Credit Mix (10%): A well-balanced financial platter, brimming with different types of credit, sends a message of responsibility and trustworthiness. Lenders prefer a diversified credit mix consisting of installment loans, secured loans, and revolving credit. Having a diverse range yet managing them mindfully is a sign that you can handle various types of debt responsibly.

5. New Credit Inquiries (10%): Every time you apply for new credit – whether it's a car loan, mortgage, or just another credit card – the lender performs a "hard inquiry" on your report. Too many hard inquiries in quick succession can ding your score as they hint at desperation or potential future financial trouble.

Consider spacing out your applications over time to minimize damage to your score from multiple inquiries. And take heart – these effects diminish over time as responsible actions overshadow past indiscretions.

CHAPTER 3
CREDIT REPORTS AND SCORES

A CREDIT REPORT PAINTS A COMPREHENSIVE PICTURE OF AN INDIVIDUAL'S CREDIT HISTORY, encompassing information on how much debt they carry, their repayment habits, and more. Credit scores are a numerical representation derived from an individual's credit report and serve as a shorthand for lenders to evaluate their creditworthiness.

Now that we know what they are, let's explore the significance of an individual's credit score. A high credit score will not only earn you favorable interest rates but also provide access to premium credit card rewards programs, lower insurance premiums, and even play a role in securing your dream job. Understanding the factors that influence your credit score is crucial to molding it into shape.

HOW TO OBTAIN YOUR CREDIT REPORT

A credit report is a detailed record of your financial history, including payment history, debts, public records, and other pertinent information. Credit bureaus compile this data and use it to calculate your credit score – an essential number that lenders consider when deciding whether to approve or deny your application for credit products.

Now that we have established the importance of a credit report let's explore the various ways to obtain one. In the United States, there are three major credit bureaus: Equifax, Experian, and TransUnion. Each bureau compiles its own version of your credit report based on information received from creditors.

Under federal law, you are entitled to one free copy of your credit report from each bureau every 12 months. It is prudent to spread these requests throughout the year as it allows you to keep tabs on any changes or suspicious activity in your reports.

To obtain your annual free credit reports from all three bureaus:

1. Visit AnnualCreditReport.com: This central website provides access to free credit reports from Equifax, Experian, and TransUnion. To request your reports online, follow the instructions provided on the website.

2. Call (877) 322-8228: Alternatively, you can request your free credit reports by phone. Be prepared with your personal information like Social Security Number (SSN), date of birth, and current address.

3. Mail your request: Using the Annual Credit Report Request Form, you can also mail a request to:

- Annual Credit Report Request Service
- P.O. Box 105281
- Atlanta, GA 30348-5281

In addition to free annual credit reports, you may also be eligible for a free report under certain circumstances such as:

1. Unemployment: If you are unemployed and plan to seek employment within the next 60 days, you qualify for a free credit report.

2. Fraud or identity theft: If you believe that fraud or identity theft has impacted your credit report, you can request free copies from all three bureaus.

3. Denied credit or insurance: If you have been denied credit or insurance within the past 60 days based on information included in your credit report, you are entitled to a free copy of the report used by the lender or insurer.

UNDERSTANDING YOUR CREDIT SCORE

A credit score is a numerical value representing your overall creditworthiness, calculated using information from your credit report. This three-digit number is like a financial health-meter, giving lenders an idea about how responsible and reliable you are when it comes to managing debt and repaying loans. The higher the score, the more financially trustworthy you seem on paper.

The most widely used credit scoring model is FICO (Fair Isaac Corporation), with scores ranging from 300 (lowest) to 850 (highest). Your FICO score is based on five essential factors: payment history (35%), amounts owed (30%), length of credit history (15%), new credit accounts (10%), and types of credit used (10%).

Lenders use your credit score to judge if lending you money is a good or risky decision. It also helps them determine the terms and interest rates that best suit your profile. Higher scores typically enable access to better loan offers and lower interest rates - so understanding how it works is vital for prudent financial management.

IMPROVING YOUR CREDIT SCORE

To maintain a high credit score and unlock the financial opportunities that come with it, follow these best practices:

1. Make timely payments: One of the most effective ways to improve your credit score is by paying your bills on time. Lenders view late payments as a red flag, so do everything you can to avoid missing payments. Set up automatic payments or set reminders in your calendar. By consistently paying your bills on time, you're demonstrating that you're a responsible borrower.

2. Keep balances low: High amounts owed can negatively impact your credit score. Aim to keep your total debt below 30% of your available credit limits. If you currently have high balances, create a plan to pay off the debt as soon as possible. Your hard work will pay dividends in the form of a better credit rating.

3. Don't close old accounts: The age of your accounts plays a significant role in determining your credit score. Closing an old account reduces your overall available credit and may shorten your credit history. Instead of closing accounts, focus on building positive payment habits.

4. Diversify your credit portfolio: Different types of credit show that you can manage various financial responsibilities. A mix of installment loans (such as car loans, student loans, or mortgages) and revolving credit (like credit cards) can create a healthier profile for prospective lenders.

5. Limit new credit inquiries: Applying for several new credit accounts in a short period signals potential lenders that you could be a high-risk borrower. Spread out your credit inquiries and keep them to a minimum. Furthermore, do your research before applying for new credit to ensure you're likely to get approved.

6. Routinely check your credit reports: Monitoring your credit allows you to catch any inaccuracies or fraudulent activity early. Request a free report from each of the major credit bureaus - Equifax, Experian, and TransUnion - once every 12 months. If you spot any discrepancies, dispute them immediately.

7. Optimize your payment strategies: Prioritize paying off high-interest debts first while still making minimum payments on other accounts. This method could save you money on interest expenses in the long run and increase your overall financial health.

Improving your credit score is achievable with patience, discipline, and commitment to good financial habits. By following these powerful strategies outlined in this section, you're one step closer to unlocking the incredible benefits that come with an excellent credit score.

BOOK TWO

CREDIT REPAIR STRATEGIES

INTRODUCTION

The second book in the CREDIT SECRETS BIBLE 5 in 1 series focuses on credit repair strategies. Delve into the process of assessing your credit situation by reviewing your credit report, identifying errors, and setting improvement goals. Learn actionable DIY techniques such as disputing inaccuracies, negotiating with creditors, and employing debt validation strategies. Finally, explore when to consider professional help and differentiate between credit repair services and credit counseling.

CHAPTER 4
ASSESSING YOUR CREDIT SITUATION

BEFORE DIVING INTO THE DETAILS, IT IS CRUCIAL TO UNDERSTAND THE COMPONENTS THAT MAKE UP your credit situation. Your credit score is a numeric representation of your creditworthiness, based on a variety of factors such as payment history, amount of debt, length of credit history, and more. By investigating these components and understanding how they contribute to your overall credit health, you can begin to take control and create a brighter financial future.

The first step in assessing your credit situation is obtaining a copy of your credit report. This document is a comprehensive summary of your borrowing and repayment history provided by one of the three major credit bureaus—Experian, Equifax, or TransUnion.

REVIEWING YOUR CREDIT REPORT

Take the time to read through each report carefully and check for any inaccuracies. Verify if all of the accounts listed belong to you, and make sure all payments have been accurately reported. Identifying errors on your report early can prevent potential damage to your credit score.

Look specifically for negative items on your report, such as charged-off accounts, late payments, or collections. These items can have a significant impact on your credit score and overall financial health. If you find any incorrect negative data on your report, it's essential to file a dispute with the respective credit reporting agency. This process may take some time and effort but will ultimately result in a more accurate portrayal of your creditworthiness.

While examining your credit report, pay special attention to outstanding debts and their age. Older debts carry less weight than newly incurred ones when determining your credit score. Recognize patterns and behaviors that may be putting you in debt – now is an excellent opportunity for reflection and change.

Understanding how much money you owe and to whom can help you create an action plan for debt repayment. Start by paying down high-interest debts first or consolidating loans to get a more favorable interest rate. Additionally, set a goal to pay off your entire credit card balance each month to avoid accumulating more debt.

One often overlooked aspect of a credit report is your credit utilization rate, which is the percentage of your total available credit being used. A high credit utilization can negatively impact your score, even if you're making all of your payments on time. Aim to keep this rate below 30% for the best possible impact on your credit score.

Reviewing your credit report is an essential step in assessing your financial health and taking control of your credit situation. Identifying patterns, correcting errors, and staying informed about the age and amount of your outstanding debts will empower you on the journey to financial freedom.

IDENTIFYING ERRORS AND ISSUES

Once you have the reports in hand, thoroughly review them for any errors or potential problems. The following are common issues found in credit reports that can negatively impact your score:

1. Incorrect personal information: Check that your name, address, Social Security number, and other personal details are correct. Reporting incorrect information may imply that someone else's negative records have been mixed with yours.

2. Duplicate accounts: If you see an account listed more than once on your report, it could significantly lower your credit score. Duplicate accounts can occur when a lender reports the same debt under different names or when debts are transferred between collection agencies.

3. Outdated information: Negative information such as late payments, charge-offs, or repossessions should be removed after seven years. Bankruptcies typically stay on for ten years.

4. Unauthorized inquiries: When a lender checks your credit without permission or justification, it's considered an unauthorized inquiry. These inquiries can lower your score and stay on for two years.

5. Fraudulent accounts: These are accounts that have been opened in your name without permission or accounts where activity isn't recognized by you. It signifies possible identity theft.

Now that you know what to look for, let's discuss the importance of resolving these errors and issues. First, identify and compile a list of all discrepancies. Make a copy of the original report and highlight the problematic areas.

Next, gather any documentation that supports your claim. This may include account statements, payment records, or identification documents like a driver's license or Social Security card.

Craft a dispute letter addressed to each credit bureau that provided a report containing the error(s). Clearly state the problem(s), explain why the information is incorrect, and request it be corrected or removed. Ensure you're professional and concise in your communication and always keep the tone respectful. Include copies (not originals) of relevant documentation to support your argument.

After mailing the dispute letter, send a similar letter to the creditor reporting the error(s), along with copies of supporting documents. The Fair Credit Reporting Act requires both credit bureaus and creditors to investigate disputes.

The credit bureaus must start an investigation within 30 days of receiving your claim. Upon completion of their inquiry (usually within 45 days), they will send you an updated copy of your credit report with resolved issues if found valid.

If the disputes are not resolved in your favor, you have a right to request that a brief statement be added to your credit report explaining your side, which lenders may take into consideration when reviewing your application for credit.

SETTING CREDIT IMPROVEMENT GOALS

Every journey starts with a single step, and the path to better credit health is no exception. In the world of personal finance, knowing where you are and where you want to go is essential to reaching your destination.

The first step to setting credit improvement goals is understanding your current financial situation. Armed with this knowledge, you can now identify areas where improvement is needed. Are there any late payments or accounts in collections? Is your credit utilization ratio (the percentage of available credit that you're using) too high? Write down all potential problem areas so that you can address them as part of your goals.

With these issues in mind, it's time to set specific, measurable targets for improvement. Consider breaking down larger goals into smaller milestones to make them more manageable and achievable. For example, if your goal is to increase your credit score by 100 points within a year, aim for a 25-point increase every three months.

You might be wondering – what kinds of goals should I set? Here are some suggestions:

1. Improve payment history: Make it a goal to pay all bills on time going forward. If you have difficulty remembering due dates or keeping track of multiple bills, set up automatic payments or calendar reminders.

2. Lower credit utilization: Aim to keep your revolving balances at no more than 30% of total available credit (preferably lower). You can achieve this by paying off existing balances or increasing credit limits.

3. Measure progress: Regularly check your credit report and monitor your credit score to see how your efforts are making a difference.

Remember to be realistic with your goals and deadlines. Improving one's credit takes time, and setbacks can occur along the way. Expecting too much too soon might lead to disappointment or giving up before seeing any significant results.

Once you've defined your credit improvement goals, it's essential to remain disciplined to achieve them. Develop a strategy that includes not only addressing past mistakes but also building positive financial habits moving forward. Consider creating a budget and tracking your expenses to ensure that you're spending within your means.

As you work towards these goals, don't forget to celebrate small victories. Recognize the progress made and reward yourself for the milestones achieved – whether that's finally paying off a collection account or seeing an increase in your credit score after months of hard work. Celebrating success can be a powerful motivator, inspiring you to continue on your path toward better credit health.

Throughout this journey, be patient and persistent. There's no magic button for boosting your credit score overnight; it takes time and dedication. But by setting clear goals, staying disciplined, and regularly reassessing your progress, you'll soon find yourself in a much stronger financial position.

CHAPTER 5
DIY CREDIT REPAIR TECHNIQUES

Have you ever looked at your credit score and cringed? In today's economy, a good credit score is essential for financial stability. Your ability to obtain loans, rent an apartment, or even get a job can all be impacted by your credit history. Fortunately, there are do-it-yourself (DIY) techniques that you can employ to repair your credit, without relying on expensive credit repair firms.

In this chapter, we will explore the key aspects of DIY credit repair techniques that can save you time and money while paving the way towards a better financial future.

DISPUTING INACCURACIES

Once you have identified the inaccuracies within your credit reports, follow these steps to remove the errors and improve your credit health:

1. Make a List of Inaccuracies: Start by compiling a complete list of errors found in the three reports. Sorting them out by dispute type can save time when contacting the reporting agencies.

2. Categorize Dispute Reasons: Classify all disputes into categories such as incorrect personal information, falsely reported late payments, charged-off accounts, or fraudulent accounts. This organization will streamline the process when you initiate communication with the agencies.

3. Gather Supporting Documentation: Gather any documents that support the dispute - proof of on-time payment, account statements, and any correspondence from creditors confirming settled or closed accounts. Having hard evidence maximizes your chances of successfully disputing inaccuracies.

4. Draft Dispute Letters: Write separate dispute letters for each reporting agency tailored to its respective report's inaccuracies. Provide clear descriptions of each mistake in a concise manner and attach copies of supporting documents for each error.

5. Send Dispute Letters via Certified Mail: Sending your letters via certified mail shows dedication and ensures the bureau's receipt. Keep copies of all correspondence to track your case efficiently.

6. Await Communication: The Credit Reporting Agencies (CRAs) have 30 days to investigate and respond to your disputes. A favorable response will reflect positively on your credit, but do not lose hope if it takes longer than expected or requires more verifications.

7. Review the Results: After receiving the bureaus' responses, review them for accuracy. If they remove or correct inaccurate information, your credit score will see a boost shortly.

8. Repeat the Process if Necessary: In some situations, you may need to provide additional information or restart the process from scratch if some errors remain unaddressed. Persistence is key in credit repair – don't be afraid to re-dispute!

Taking ownership of your credit health and actively disputing inaccuracies can vastly improve your financial standing and increase your access to attractive loans, mortgages, or lines of credit. Moreover, higher credit scores afford favorable terms when applying for these instruments.

Remember that maintaining good financial habits will keep inaccuracies from reappearing in your reports. Consistent on-time payments and staying within healthy credit utilization ratios allow you to reap extensive benefits in the long run.

NEGOTIATING WITH CREDITORS

It happens to the best of us – a financially challenging event occurs, we miss a payment or two, and our credit score takes a hit. In moments like these, despair may set in. However, you can't let your past mistakes hold you back forever. With the correct DIY credit repair technique, specifically negotiating with creditors, anyone can address their credit hiccups and work their way back to financial stability.

1. Assess Your Situation: Before reaching out to your creditors, take an honest look at your current financial standing. Review your credit report and identify all outstanding debts and late payments. This information will help you plan your negotiation strategy more effectively.

2. Prioritize Your Debts: Not all debts are created equal. Some have more significant impacts on your overall credit score than others. Prioritize the most crucial debts first—such as those with high interest rates or those that have been overdue for an extended period.

3. Reach Out to Creditors: Once you have a clear picture of your financial situation, it's time to open lines of communication with your creditors. Be polite and honest during these conversations; remember that they are more likely to help if you treat them respectfully.

4. Make an Offer: In many cases, creditors are willing to negotiate a reduced payment amount or even wipe out some of the debt in exchange for a lump sum payment. Consider offering them a compromise that is fair for both parties. If you don't feel comfortable doing this on your own, seek assistance from a trusted friend or family member.

5. Get Everything in Writing: Once you've reached an agreement with your creditors, make sure everything is documented in writing. This step is crucial, as it will serve as evidence if any disputes arise in the future.

6. Set Up a Payment Plan: If you cannot afford a lump sum payment, many creditors are happy to work with you to create a manageable payment plan. Be honest about what you can realistically afford each month and stick to the agreed-upon amount.

7. Stay Committed: The path to financial freedom takes dedication. To ensure your credit repair effort is successful, make your payments on time or even ahead of schedule, reduce your overall debt load, and avoid taking on new debt that could jeopardize your progress.

Negotiating with creditors can be an intimidating process, but it's essential to remember that these companies want to get paid as much as you want to improve your credit score. If you approach the situation with patience, persistence, and professionalism, there's a good chance that your creditors will be more than willing to work with you.

DEBT VALIDATION STRATEGIES

If financial troubles have left you with less-than-stellar credit, don't fret! One of the most powerful and cost-effective methods within this DIY manual is the debt validation strategy. By mastering this technique, you'll regain control of your financial wellbeing and chart a course towards a bright, debt-free future.

Debt validation is a process in which you legally challenge the validity of a debt that has been assigned to you. More often than not, numerous errors can be found in the reporting process, making the demand for payment impossible to uphold. Under federal law - specifically, the Fair Debt Collection Practices Act (FDCPA) - consumers possess the right to request validation of debts from collectors. Staying well-informed about these rights positions you to hold lenders accountable and correct unjust records.

So, where should you begin? Follow these five steps for implementing a successful debt validation strategy:

1. Review your credit report: You can access your full credit report for free once every 12 months by visiting AnnualCreditReport.com. Closely review each detail in search of discrepancies – late payments that never occurred or delinquencies from unknown sources, for example. It's crucial that you identify any errors at this stage.

2. Send a debt validation letter: Upon discovering inaccuracies in your report, send a debt validation letter to the collection agency responsible (see our sample letter in Chapter 3). A crucial point to remember when drafting this correspondence is timeliness – ensure it's postmarked within 30 days of learning about the collection attempts concerning the disputed debt. Your letter should state clearly that you're disputing their claim and request them to validate the amount owed.

3. Await their response: Once your debt validation letter reaches its destination, under the FDCPA, the collection agency must cease any further contact until they can verify the debt. This includes halting credit reporting and, potentially, removing any negative credit entries from your report.

4. Analyze the evidence: Upon receiving verification from the collector, carefully examine their documentation to determine if it substantiates their claim to the debt. It's not uncommon for agencies to lack accurate records or provide unreliable information, so leaving no stone unturned is essential. If you suspect that they have failed to prove their case, dispute their evidence and reiterate your request for proper validation.

5. Follow up with credit bureaus: After the completion of this process or the expiration of the 30-day response window (whichever occurs first), send a letter to each credit reporting bureau referencing the disputed debt (samples in Chapter 4). Attach copies of your correspondence with the collection agency as well as any documents associated with your credit dispute. Request that they investigate and rectify your record accordingly.

By mastering this DIY technique, you enable yourself to challenge unjust debts and regain control of your credit score. A strong understanding of your rights combined with tactical persistence creates a formidable defense against collection agencies and their attempts to profit from misinformation.

Reinvention is an ongoing journey - and "Credit Secrets Bible" serves as a reliable roadmap to guide you in achieving a healthy financial state. This resource offers invaluable insights into protecting your finances and leveraging key strategies for timely credit repair. As you progress through these pages, we hope your confidence grows tenfold, proving that even in times of disarray, there's always the possibility for redemption.

CHAPTER 6
PROFESSIONAL CREDIT REPAIR SERVICES

WITH THE EVER-GROWING IMPORTANCE OF GOOD CREDIT, THE DEMAND FOR PROFESSIONAL CREDIT repair services has skyrocketed. These experts, armed with a wealth of knowledge found in books like the Credit Secrets Bible, work tirelessly to help clients improve their credit scores and regain financial freedom.

But what exactly is a professional credit repair service? And how can they help you triumph over bad credit, banishing it back to the shadows from whence it came?

When you enlist the help of a professional credit repair service, you're partnering with an experienced team that specializes in identifying errors on your credit report, disputing inaccuracies with credit bureaus, and negotiating with creditors on your behalf. With years of experience under their belts, these experts understand the intricacies of the financial system and possess insider knowledge on how to successfully challenge incorrect information.

One might wonder why they should hire a professional when they could undertake these tasks themselves. While it's true that many people choose to navigate the treacherous waters of credit repair alone, mistakes made in this process can have long-lasting consequences. Incorrectly disputing items on your report may lead to legal action or further harm to your score—a risk not worth taking for most people.

Professional credit repair services employ a multi-step approach that includes:

1. Evaluation: The first step is assessing your current financial situation and identifying any errors or inaccuracies present on your credit report.

2. Disputes: The professionals then compile evidence supporting each dispute and submit requests to have inaccuracies removed or corrected.

3. Negotiation: After successful disputes, the team negotiates with creditors to remove additional negative information from your report.

4. Education and Coaching: Finally, they provide you with personalized advice on how to maintain good credit moving forward.

While credit repair may seem like a journey with an impossible end, experienced professionals have a proven track record of success. Patience and persistence are key in this process, as results may take time. However, even small improvements to your credit score can make a substantial difference in your financial outlook.

WHEN TO CONSIDER PROFESSIONAL HELP

before you dive headfirst into tackling those past financial mistakes, take a moment to consider whether or not professional credit repair services might be the best option for you. It's important to know when to turn to professional help in order to avoid worsening your situation.

First and foremost, the primary goal of credit repair agencies is to identify discrepancies in your credit report, dispute them, and ultimately work towards a higher credit score. While some individuals may want to take matters into their own hands, there are specific situations where professional help would be more beneficial.

1. Lack of Time and Expertise: Navigating through dense information and tedious processes can be overwhelming for someone without adequate experience. If you're feeling unsure about how to address errors in your credit report or if you simply do not have the time to devote to understanding and rectifying these issues, hiring a professional is a wise choice.

2. Multiple Credit Issues: When dealing with multiple financial snags negatively impacting your credit score, it's essential to identify the root causes and strategize accordingly. If you're overwhelmed by numerous imperfections on your report, a credit repair service will be equipped with the necessary tools and expertise to guide you through the process and prioritize which issues should be addressed first.

3. Complicated Credit Problems: If you're dealing with complex situations such as bankruptcy, identity theft, or legal disputes affecting your credit score, it's crucial to seek professional guidance. In cases like these, a reputable credit repair service will have experience navigating these tricky scenarios efficiently and confidently.

4. Miscommunication with Creditors or Bureaus: If you've attempted DIY credit repair but found yourself tangled in miscommunications with creditors or bureaus, consulting professionals can alleviate the stress and streamline communications. Their experience allows them to advocate on your behalf, often leading to faster resolutions and better outcomes.

5. You've Tried and Failed on Your Own: There's no shame in admitting that you've tackled your credit repair solo but haven't seen the desired results. In fact, acknowledging this is a crucial step toward finding the right solution for your credit journey. If you've tried a DIY approach with little success, it may be time to connect with a professional who can offer more targeted strategies.

When seeking professional help, it's crucial to conduct thorough research and choose a reputable service or individual with a track record of success. Ensure that they are knowledgeable about the various credit reporting laws such as the Fair Credit Reporting Act (FCRA), the Fair Debt Collection Practices Act (FDCPA), and the Credit Repair Organizations Act (CROA).

Remember, credit repair agencies vary in terms of price and performance. Compare different companies' offerings, read customer reviews, and ask for recommendations from friends or family members who utilized professional credit repair services. After you've narrowed down potential prospects, consult with each one to appropriately assess their qualifications and compatibility with your specific situation.

CHOOSING A CREDIT REPAIR COMPANY

With so much importance placed on credit, it's no wonder people are increasingly turning to credit repair companies to help improve their scores and pave the way for brighter financial futures. But how do you choose the right company to trust with such a critical task?

Let's explore the process of selecting a reputable credit repair company and provide you with key considerations to keep in mind as you make your decision.

1. Research the Company's Experience and Reputation: Begin your search for a credit repair company by looking at their years of experience in the industry and any certifications they may hold, such as accreditation with the Better Business Bureau (BBB). Investigate their online presence, explore their website, check out customer testimonials, and read unbiased reviews on various review websites. Look for mentions of any legal troubles or complaints filed against them. Be wary of companies that make outrageous claims or guarantee specific results—no one can promise specific outcomes when it comes to repairing credit.

2. Understand the Range of Services Offered: Different credit repair companies offer varying services designed to help consumers improve their credit scores. Some may focus on disputing errors on your credit report, while others might offer assistance in negotiating with creditors or developing personalized financial plans. Assess your unique situation and align your needs with the services provided by each prospective company. Make sure they cater to your individual requirements as you select the best-suited company for your situation.

3. Assess Their Fee Structure: Credit repair services can come at a cost—often in the form of upfront fees, monthly fees, or both. Prioritize transparency as you evaluate potential companies' fee structures. Avoid credit repair organizations that charge for services before they deliver results, as this could be a red flag that they may not follow through on their promises. Instead, opt for companies that are open about their pricing and provide straightforward explanations of the costs associated with their services.

4. Inquire About Client Support: Throughout the credit repair process, it's essential to have access to responsive and knowledgeable client support. Inquire about each company's communication methods (phone, email, chat) and their availability for answering questions regarding your case. The best credit repair organizations will be staffed by professionals who can address your concerns.

5. Assess Their Cancellation Policy: It is crucial to know whether or not a credit repair company offers a money-back guarantee or cancellation policy that allows you to end the contract without any fees if you are dissatisfied with their service. A reputable organization should offer flexible and accommodating cancellation options that prioritize customer satisfaction and trust.

6. Seek Referrals from Trusted Sources: Lastly, consider seeking recommendations from friends, family members, or financial advisers who have successfully utilized credit repair services in the past. Honest referrals can provide insights into the company's capabilities and help guide your decision-making process.

CREDIT REPAIR VS. CREDIT COUNSELING

Two key methods through which you can regain control over your financial life are credit repair and credit counseling. Both of these approaches can help you improve your credit score and financial health, but they are different in terms of their goals and the strategies they employ. This chapter aims to guide you in understanding the differences between credit repair and credit counseling and help you decide which method best suits your needs.

1. Credit Repair: Credit repair involves the process of identifying errors or discrepancies in your credit report and taking steps to correct them. A professional performing this task scrutinizes your report thoroughly in search of inaccuracies that might adversely affect your score, such as outdated information, duplicate entries, or false details about late payments.

Once the errors have been spotted, a credit repair professional liaises with the relevant authorities on your behalf to challenge the inaccurate data and request its rectification. To maximize the effectiveness of this process, you must provide supporting documentation proving the errors in question.

The ultimate goal of credit repair is to boost your credit score by removing inaccurate information that has a negative impact on it. Since an improved score opens up better financial opportunities for people, you may find that engaging a credit repair expert is a rewarding investment.

2. Credit Counseling: Credit counseling takes a broader approach than solely focusing on repairing your existing credit report. It comprises various strategies designed to assist clients with debt management, budgeting, financial education, and learning better money habits.

A credit counselor starts their work by helping you assess your overall financial situation. They examine your income sources, expenses, assets, liabilities and delve into any specific issues like high-interest debt or poor spending habits. Their analysis generates insights that are used to develop a personalized financial management plan tailored towards your needs.

These professionals also negotiate with creditors in an effort to secure lower interest rates, waive fees, or make any other concessions that benefit your financial well-being. Additionally, they provide regular guidance and support throughout your journey to better credit health.

The decision to engage in credit repair or credit counseling largely depends on your personal circumstances, goals, and priorities. Here are some factors to consider when making a choice:

1. Urgency: If you need to improve your credit score quickly, credit repair is a more suitable option since it focuses on removing negative items from your report.

2. Debt levels: If managing high levels of debt has become overwhelming and you could use professional help in consolidating loans or negotiating more favorable terms with creditors, then credit counseling is likely the way to go.

3. Financial education: If you need guidance in managing your finances more effectively and want to acquire better money habits that will serve you long-term, consider enlisting the expertise of a credit counselor for comprehensive ongoing assistance.

4. Scope of Issues: If your main concern is clearing up inaccuracies on your report, credit repair is more targeted at achieving this goal. However, if you face broader financial challenges in managing debt, creating budgets, or setting financial goals, credit counseling provides a holistic solution addressing all these concerns.

BOOK THREE

CREDIT MANAGEMENT AND DEBT REDUCTION

INTRODUCTION

In this third installment of the CREDIT SECRETS BIBLE 5 in 1 series, you'll discover valuable information on managing your credit effectively and reducing debt through budgeting, smart credit card use, and debt consolidation. Learn the importance of a credit-friendly budget, managing expenses wisely, and tips for building positive habits that will improve your overall financial health.

CHAPTER 7
BUDGETING FOR BETTER CREDIT

BUDGETING IS THE PROCESS OF ALLOCATING YOUR INCOME TO VARIOUS EXPENSES IN A SYSTEMATIC AND organized manner. To begin the journey of improving your credit through smart budgeting, you must first understand your financial situation. Calculate your monthly take-home income and identify fixed and variable expenses in order to create a baseline. Fixed expenses include rent or mortgage payments, utility bills, and insurance premiums, while variable expenses may change from month to month, such as groceries, entertainment or travel costs.

From these calculations, devise a monthly budget that takes into account all your expenses. Maintain an emergency fund and allocate a percentage of your income towards savings or investments. The purpose of creating this budget is not only to control your spending but also to pay off existing debts on time, avoid taking on excessive high-interest loans, and prevent damage to your credit score.

Once you have established a budget, it is crucial to monitor and update it regularly. As life changes or unexpected expenses arise, make adjustments accordingly. A well-maintained budget is key to achieving financial success and better credit health.

CREATING A CREDIT-FRIENDLY BUDGET

A well-planned budget is the key to strengthening your credit and securing your financial future. Let's delve into creating a credit-friendly budget that will not only help improve your credit score but also enable you to develop responsible financial habits.

1. Assess Your Financial Situation: The first step in creating a credit-friendly budget is assessing your financial situation. To do this, you need to gather all your financial statements, including bank accounts, credit card statements, investment accounts, and loan documents. Record your income from various sources and calculate your average monthly earnings.

Next, list all your fixed expenses such as rent or mortgage payments, insurance premiums, and utilities. Separately record variable expenses such as food, clothing, transportation, entertainment, and medical bills. Don't forget to include annual payments and other irregular expenses that pop up throughout the year.

2. Evaluate Your Income-to-Debt Ratio: Understanding the relationship between your income and debt is crucial in creating a budget that is both sustainable and credit-friendly. Your income-to-debt ratio is calculated by dividing your monthly debt payments by your monthly gross income.

A higher ratio indicates that you are spending too much on debt repayment compared to your earnings – which could signal trouble when it comes to seeking new credit lines or better interest rates on existing loans. Aim for a lower ratio (below 36%) where possible.

3. Set Realistic Goals: Now that you know the state of your finances, it's time to set goals for improving them! Start by deciding what you want to achieve over three to six months or even a year – reducing debt, building an emergency fund for unexpected expenses, improving your credit score or achieving specific financial milestones.

Ensure the goals are specific, measurable, and attainable – setting unrealistic goals could lead to frustration and temptation to abandon the budget completely.

4. Pay off Debts Strategically: It's important to prioritize tackling high-interest debt first, as it has a significant impact on your credit score and overall financial health. Focus on strategies such as the debt avalanche method (starting with the highest interest rate debts) or the snowball technique (starting with the smallest debts) to pay off debts efficiently.

Make sure to take advantage of available resources such as debt consolidation offers or balance transfer options that can help reduce interest rates and simplify monthly payments.

5. Establish a Contingency Fund: Creating a safety net for unexpected expenses is crucial in developing a budget that promotes healthy credit habits. Set aside three to six months' worth of living expenses in an emergency fund – this not only helps avoid taking on new debt in times of crisis but also signals responsible financial management to creditors.

6. Autopay for Recurring Bills: Automating regular bill payments can be an effective way to ensure timely payments and avoid accumulating unnecessary late fees or extra interest charges – factors that could hurt your credit score.

7. Stick to Your Budget and Monitor Progress: A credit-friendly budget requires discipline and diligence. Regularly track your spending against what you've allocated for each category, adjusting allocations as necessary to ensure you don't overspend.

Review your budget every month, making adjustments where needed or adjusting goals where necessary – this not only keeps you accountable but helps adapt your budget according to changing circumstances.

By proactively monitoring expenses, setting realistic goals, and paying off debts strategically, you'll forge a strong foundation for a stable financial future while also enjoying the benefits that come with an improved credit score. Remember, the journey towards a better credit score and financial freedom starts with creating a budget that supports your goals and encourages good habits.

MANAGING EXPENSES EFFECTIVELY

The first step towards effectively managing your expenses is to understand where your money is going. Make a list of all your recurring expenses, such as rent or mortgage payments, utilities, loan payments, and insurance premiums. Additionally, it's crucial to track your day-to-day spending on items like groceries, dining out, entertainment, and clothing.

To assist with this process, consider using budgeting tools or apps that automatically categorize and track your spending. Regularly reviewing these categories will enable you to spot trends in your expenses and identify areas where you may be overspending.

1. Cutting Down Unnecessary Expenses: After gaining a clear picture of your current expenses, it's time to pinpoint the areas where you can save money. While some costs may seem trivial individually, they add up over time. Here are a few ideas for cutting down on unnecessary expenses:

1. *Cancel unused subscriptions:* Gym memberships, video streaming services, or magazine subscriptions that are not being used should be canceled to save money each month.
2. *Shop smarter:* Search for discounts or sales before making purchases and learn the art of haggling for big-ticket items.
3. *Cook at home:* Eating out regularly can be a significant expense; cooking at home is often more cost-effective and healthier.
4. *Seek lower-cost alternatives for entertainment:* Attend free local events or search for activities that offer unlimited fun without continuous spending.

By identifying these areas and taking control of your spending habits, you'll begin to see a noticeable improvement in your finances over time.

2. Creating an Emergency Fund: Life is full of surprises, and unfortunately, many of them can be expensive. Unforeseen events like car repairs, medical emergencies, or job loss can wreak havoc on your financial stability. Therefore, it's crucial to establish an emergency fund to provide a safety net for these situations.

Aim to save at least three to six months' worth of living expenses. Start by setting aside a small portion of your income each month, and as you become more comfortable with your budget, increase that amount.

3. Sticking to a Budget: Creating and adhering to a well-planned budget is the backbone of managing expenses effectively. List your monthly income from all sources and subtract your fixed and variable expenses. Before spending any money on non-essential items or luxuries, be sure to allocate adequate funds to essential expenses and saving goals.

Monitoring your budget regularly helps keep you accountable for your spending decisions and allows you to make adjustments when necessary. The key to a successful budget is consistency – it's not about depriving yourself of enjoyment but rather making informed decisions that help guarantee financial security in the long run.

4. Making Timely Payments: One of the most significant contributors to negative credit scores is late payments. Failing to pay bills on time can result in late fees and interest charges, which not only hurt your finances but also damage your credit history.

To avoid these consequences, set up automatic payments for all recurring expenses like rent, utilities, or subscriptions. Additionally, create reminders for other important dates such as credit card payments or property taxes.

SAVINGS STRATEGIES

In the quest to achieve financial security and success, having a well-defined savings strategy is just as important as maintaining a good credit score. This section will reveal proven savings methods that can lead you on the path toward financial freedom. By taking the necessary steps to build your savings, you'll be better equipped to meet financial emergencies and realize your big life goals.

1. Setting Financial Goals: The first step in saving money intelligently is having a clear understanding of your short-term and long-term financial goals. This could include saving for a new car, paying off your mortgage early, or planning for retirement. Write down these goals and revisit them regularly to stay focused and motivated.

2. Create a Realistic Budget: Once you have set your financial goals, determine how much you need to save each month. Develop a budget based on your income and expenses, allocating specific amounts for each of your goals. Identify areas where you can cut costs and remember to differentiate between needs and wants.

3. Establish an Emergency Fund: A vital step in achieving financial stability is building an emergency fund to cover unexpected expenses such as medical emergencies, car repairs, or job loss. Ideally, this fund should have enough money to cover three to six months' worth of living expenses. Having an emergency fund will help you avoid relying on credit cards or loans during times of crisis and keep your credit score intact.

4. Use High-Interest Savings Accounts: Traditional savings accounts offer minimal interest rates, which are often lower than inflation rates. That's why it's essential to consider high-interest savings accounts when building your nest egg. These accounts provide more substantial returns on your deposits while maintaining easy access to your funds.

5. Automate Your Savings: To ensure consistency in saving month after month, set up an automatic transfer from your paycheck or checking account into your savings account. By automating this process, you will eliminate the need for self-discipline and will consistently prioritize savings without any extra effort.

6. Save Windfalls and Bonuses: If you receive an unexpected financial gain, consider using this money to boost your savings instead of spending it all at once. Bonuses, tax refunds, and inheritances are prime examples of windfalls that can significantly benefit your savings goals when used wisely.

7. Pay Off High-Interest Debt: Having high-interest debt can derail your efforts to save money due to the interest payments eating away at your income. Aim to pay off high-interest loans and credit card balances as soon as possible before allocating more money towards savings.

8. Take Advantage of Employer Retirement Plans: Many companies offer employer-sponsored retirement plans such as 401(k) or 403(b), which allow you to contribute pre-tax income towards your retirement investments. Additionally, some employers offer contribution matching, which maximizes the amount of money added to your account each year. Be sure to take full advantage of these programs to supplement your long-term savings strategy.

9. Develop Passive Income Streams: One effective way to increase your savings potential is by developing passive income streams. This could include rental income from real estate investments, royalties from creative works, or dividends from stocks and mutual funds. Passive income can provide you with a steady source of additional funds to allocate towards your savings goals.

10. Find Creative Ways to Save: A great method for saving more is discovering and utilizing creative strategies that suit your lifestyle:

- Consider using cash-back apps or credit cards that reward points converted into actual savings.

- Try the "pay yourself first" method by setting aside a specific percentage of each paycheck before budgeting other expenses.
- Join a savings challenge with friends or family members where everyone contributes a particular amount every month toward a shared goal.

Remember, achieving financial freedom takes consistency, patience, and discipline. Some sacrifices may be necessary, but in the end, a robust savings strategy will yield positive results. By incorporating these strategies into your personal financial plan, you will gradually accumulate wealth and experience the lasting benefits of a firm financial foundation.

CHAPTER 8
SMART CREDIT CARD MANAGEMENT

CREDIT CARDS—THOSE MAGICAL PIECES OF PLASTIC THAT ALLOW US TO MAKE PURCHASES NOW AND PAY later—have become indispensable in our day-to-day lives. They simplify shopping experiences, enable emergency expenditure funds, and may even help you build a good credit history if utilized responsibly. However, the pitfalls of mishandling credit cards have left many trapped in a vortex of debt—with interest rates and fees swiftly snowballing into an unending struggle to get back on track.

USING CREDIT CARDS WISELY

Every day, millions of people use credit cards as a convenient way to make purchases, build their credit score, and even manage their finances. However, if not used responsibly, credit cards can lead to substantial debt, damaged credit ratings, and financial distress. Let's explore strategies and best practices for using credit cards wisely so you can reap the benefits without suffering the consequences.

1. Understanding your credit card agreement: Before using your credit card, it's crucial to understand its terms and conditions. This includes interest rates, fees, grace periods, minimum payments, and the method of calculating interest charges. Familiarize yourself with these details to avoid unexpected charges and penalties.

2. Choosing the right credit card: With countless credit cards available in the market today, it's essential to choose the one best suited for your needs and financial goals. Consider factors such as interest rates, reward programs, annual fees, balance transfer options, and other added perks when comparing cards. Opt for a card that aligns well with your spending habits and provides benefits you'll actually use.

3. Regular tracking of your expenses: Monitoring your spending is a critical component of using credit cards wisely. Track your purchases closely by reviewing monthly statements and online transactions regularly. You can also set up account alerts for specific spending limits or unusual activity to stay in control of your finances.

4. Paying off your balance every month: Credit card debt often snowballs into unmanageable amounts due to high-interest rates on outstanding balances. Pay off your entire balance every month to avoid paying exorbitant interest charges and reduce the risk of falling into debt. Set reminders or automate payments to ensure you never miss a due date.

5. Creating a budget: A budget helps you determine how much you can afford to put on your credit card each month without overspending. Establish a plan for your expenses and stick to it, carefully considering whether each purchase is necessary and within your budget. If you find yourself consistently exceeding your limit, reevaluate your budget and cut back on non-essential expenses.

6. Setting credit card limits: Setting a limit on your credit card spending can stop excessive use and impulsive purchases. Many credit card issuers allow you to set up customizable alerts or even place temporary holds on your cards in the case of overspending.

7. Utilizing reward programs efficiently: Maximize the benefits of your credit card by using available rewards and incentives strategically. This may include cashback, travel points, or other rewards that add value to your financial life. However, be cautious not to overspend for the sake of earning rewards; the benefits likely won't outweigh the potential debt.

8. Protecting against fraud: Credit card fraud cannot only lead to unauthorized charges but also have long-lasting effects on your credit score. Safeguard your credit card information by practicing safe online shopping habits, regularly monitoring your accounts for suspicious activity, and reporting any unauthorized transactions immediately.

9. Responsible use of balance transfers: Balance transfer offers with low-interest rates may seem like a solution to overwhelming debt but can lead to more financial troubles if not used responsibly. Only utilize balance transfers if you have a plan in place to pay off the debt before the promotional period ends, as once it does, interest rates often skyrocket.

10. Maintaining good credit utilization ratio: Your credit utilization ratio is the proportion of available credit being used at any given time. A low ratio is typically seen as responsible credit card usage by lenders and positively impacts your credit score. Aim to keep this ratio below 30% to showcase financial stability and reliability.

PAYING OFF CREDIT CARD DEBT

Shrouded in a veil of secrecy and often perceived as an embarrassing financial taboo, credit card debt can feel like an insurmountable obstacle. Yet, the road to financial freedom is paved with small, consistent steps that eventually lead to complete mastery over one's credit card debt. Here are the secrets to paying off credit card debt in a strategic and efficient manner.

1. Know Where You Stand: The first step to tackling credit card debt is to take stock of your current financial situation. List all your outstanding debts, including credit cards, loans, and any other financial obligations you owe. Make note of the balance, monthly payment, and interest rate for each account. This bird's-eye view of your finances will help you recognize the magnitude of your debt and provide a baseline for tracking your progress.

2. Create A Budget: Budgeting is a powerful weapon in your fight against credit card debt. Develop a comprehensive budget that accommodates all aspects of your life, from food to leisure activities. Allocate amounts for each spending category and commit to adhering to those limits. By maintaining a strict grip on your cash flow, you will prevent additional debt from accumulating while freeing up funds to pay off your existing balances.

3. Prioritize Your Debts: Once your budget is established and you've identified discretionary funds that can be applied towards paying off credit card debt, it's time to prioritize which debts to tackle first. Two popular methods for ordering payoffs include the snowball method (focusing on the smallest balance first) and the avalanche method (focusing on the highest interest rate first). Neither approach is universally superior; choose the one that fits your personal circumstances and motivates you most.

4. Negotiate with Creditors: You may not realize it, but you can leverage your willingness to pay off debt as a bargaining chip. Reach out to your creditors and attempt to negotiate better terms on your accounts. Some people have been successful in lowering interest rates, reducing minimum payments, or even settling a portion of the debt for a lesser amount. There's no guarantee that every creditor will entertain negotiation, but it's certainly worth exploring.

5. Consider Debt Consolidation: If juggling multiple credit card debts seems overwhelming, debt consolidation may be an effective solution. This approach involves transferring all outstanding debts onto one or more lower-interest credit cards or taking out a low-interest loan to pay off the debts in full. While debt consolidation can simplify your financial landscape and save on interest costs, it is crucial to remain disciplined and not rack up new debt in the process.

6. Automate Your Payments: Maintaining a consistent payment schedule is critical to chipping away at credit card debt. To avoid missing due dates or making partial payments, automate your payments by setting up recurring transfers from your checking account to your creditors. This will eliminate human error and ensure you make steady progress towards becoming debt-free.

7. Hack Your Debt Payoffs: Small lifestyle adjustments can yield significant results when applied strategically to your debt repayments. Consider applying windfalls, such as bonuses or tax refunds, entirely towards your outstanding balances. Additionally, try implementing frugal tactics like cutting back on non-essential expenses or starting a side hustle to generate extra income.

8. Celebrate Your Milestones: Finally, take time to recognize and appreciate the milestones you achieve in paying off credit card debt. Whether it's eliminating a balance entirely or crossing another hundred dollars off the list, acknowledging these victories can boost morale and further motivate you to forge ahead with gusto.

BUILDING POSITIVE CREDIT CARD HABITS

The power to build a strong credit history lies in the palm of your hands, literally, in the form of a credit card. This tiny plastic tool, when used effectively, can pave the way to new opportunities, better financial prospects, and a financially secure life. Let's explore how to develop and maintain positive credit card habits that will lay the foundation for your future success.

1. Choose Wisely: The first step toward building good credit card habits is selecting the right card. Research and compare available options based on factors like interest rates, fees, rewards programs, and overall compatibility with your spending patterns. Opt for one with low fees and interest rates while providing excellent rewards.

2. Set Realistic Limits: To avoid drowning in debt or damaging your credit score, establish responsible spending limits on your cards. Make it a personal rule not to spend more than 30% of your available credit on each card to maintain a healthy credit utilization ratio.

3. Timely Payments: One of the most crucial habits for a strong credit foundation is punctuality in paying your bills. Pay off your balances in full and on time every month, as this demonstrates responsibility and earns you substantial points in the eyes of creditors.

4. Keep Track of Your Spending: Actively monitoring your expenses serves as an effective way to stay within budget while avoiding impulsive purchases. Create a monthly spending plan that allocates specific amounts towards saving or disposable income separate from necessities like groceries and bills.

5. Be Cautious with Cash Advances: Cash advances are tempting, but they come at a high price as they are usually associated with exorbitant interest rates and fees. Steer clear of relying on cash advances except for emergencies.

6. Know Your Grace Period: Leverage the grace period offered by most carriers between purchase dates and payment due dates. Understand this timeframe as it provides you with the ability to pay off your balance without accumulating interest charges.

7. Regularly Monitor Your Credit Report: Obtain and review your credit report every year from all three major credit bureaus (Equifax, Experian, and TransUnion). Doing so allows you to detect and dispute any errors promptly, keeping your score in the best shape possible.

8. Utilize Rewards Programs: Take full advantage of reward programs and benefits offered by credit card providers, but don't let them dictate your spending habits. Look for cards that align with your lifestyle and preferences to maximize cash back, air miles, or other available perks.

9. Maintain a Healthy Credit Mix: Display financial responsibility by using various types of credit without overextending yourself. Lenders view a diverse credit mix – comprising loans, mortgages, and multiple credit cards in balance – favorably since it showcases your ability to handle various forms of credit.

10. Address Issues Swiftly: Whenever you encounter issues pertaining to your credit cards – whether they involve a billing error or identity theft concern – act fast. The sooner you resolve problems, the less likely they are to impact your credit negatively.

11. Play the Long Game: Closing old accounts may seem like a good idea, but consider keeping longstanding cards with positive payment histories open as they contribute significantly towards building a high credit score.

With these positive habits in place, you pave the way for a remarkable financial journey. Cultivate these practices into daily routines to construct a robust credit foundation able to withstand life's inevitable hurdles while boosting your opportunities for prosperity.

CHAPTER 9
DEBT REDUCTION AND CONSOLIDATION

Debt reduction and consolidation involves strategically amalgamating your various debts into one manageable payment with reduced interest rates. The notion here is simple - to help you gain control over your finances and liberate yourself from the shackles of debt. But why should debt reduction even be on your radar? Truth be told, the vast majority are somehow engulfed in the tempest of staggering credit card balances and mountains of loans.

The very first step towards comprehending the benefits of this strategy is knowing the difference between secured and unsecured debt. Secured debts are backed by collateral, such as your home or car. Failure to repay these loans may result in repossession or foreclosure. Unsecured debts, on the other hand, do not involve collateral but come with higher interest rates due to increased risk for lenders; examples include credit card debt or medical bills.

The primary goal behind debt reduction and consolidation is to convert high-interest unsecured debts into lower-interest secured loans. By doing so, you may significantly reduce your monthly payments as well as lower your overall interest charges throughout the loan's tenure.

STRATEGIES FOR PAYING DOWN DEBT

Debt can sure feel like an ominous cloud hanging over your life, casting its dark shadows on your financial well-being. In this section, we're going to learn multiple strategies that will help you pay down your debt efficiently and bring the sunshine back into your life.

1. The Snowball Method: Made popular by financial guru Dave Ramsey, the snowball method is a psychologically gratifying way of paying off debts. To begin, list down all your debts from smallest to largest in terms of the amount owed. Start making minimum payments on all debts except the smallest one. Attack that little guy with everything you've got—throw every extra penny towards this debt. Once you've paid it off, move on to the next smallest debt and repeat. The satisfaction of eliminating each debt fuels motivation and propels your momentum further.

2. The Avalanche Method: The difference between the snowball method and the avalanche method lies in the order in which you tackle your debts. In the avalanche method, you prioritize paying off debts with the highest interest rates first. This strategy saves more money in interest payments over time.

Make a list of all debts from highest to lowest interest rate and start working your way down. Continue making minimum payments on all debts, but focus on aggressively paying off those with higher interest rates first. This disciplined approach may not satisfy as quickly as watching smaller balances disappear with the snowball method, but it's undeniably efficient.

3. Balance Transfer: Leveraging balance transfers can be an incredibly effective way to pay down high-interest credit card debt faster. Many credit card providers offer 0% APR balance transfer opportunities for a specified period (usually 6-18 months). By transferring your high-interest debt to a card with no interest, you give yourself some breathing room. This allows you to concentrate on paying down the principal balance without accruing additional interest.

Keep in mind that there are often fees and restrictions associated with these offers, so do your research and make sure it's the right fit for your needs. It's also worth noting that balance transfers should not be treated as a free pass for spending. Practice discipline and avoid adding to your debt while working towards financial freedom.

4. Debt Consolidation Loans: Often, juggling multiple loan repayment schedules can turn into a confusing mess. A consolidation loan combines several debts into one manageable payment at a lower interest rate, making it easier to budget for and pay down your debt.

You'll still be responsible for paying off the full amount, but sometimes the overall costs can be significantly reduced. However, exercise caution when considering this approach—some predatory lenders target people seeking debt consolidation, so always perform thorough due diligence before signing any agreements.

5. Trim Expenses and Increase Income: Reducing overall expenditure can fast-track your debt repayment journey. Examine your spending habits and implement a stringent budget that cuts unnecessary costs. Monitor finances closely and redirect any savings to repayments. Supplementing your income through side jobs or selling personal items can further contribute to faster repayments, ultimately leading to freedom from debt.

DEBT CONSOLIDATION OPTIONS

Debt consolidation is one of the most popular and effective strategies for dealing with high-interest debt. Here are various options for consolidating your debt, helping you make informed decisions to regain control of your finances and eventually achieve a debt-free lifestyle.

1. Balance Transfer Credit Cards: Balance transfer credit cards allow you to move your existing high-interest balances to a single card with a lower interest rate. In many cases, these cards offer an introductory period of 0% interest, which can last from 12 to 24 months. Transferring your balances to such a card can save you a considerable amount in interest while making it easier to manage your debts. The trick is to consistently pay off your balance before the promotional period ends so that you don't incur more interest charges.

2. Debt Consolidation Loans: Debt consolidation loans combine multiple debts into one loan. Typically, these loans offer lower interest rates than what you're paying on your existing debts, and they only require one monthly payment instead of multiple ones. Some lenders also offer flexible repayment plans tailored to fit your budget. Debt consolidation loans work best if you have multiple high-interest debts, like credit card balances or personal loans.

3. Home Equity Loans: A home equity loan enables you to borrow against the equity in your home for consolidating debt. In essence, these loans convert your existing unsecured debt into a secured debt backed by your property. Home equity loans often come with lower interest rates than other types of unsecured loans because they are considered less risky for lenders.

However, it's essential to remember that by using a home equity loan, you're putting your property at risk if you don't make payments on time. Hence, only choose this option if you're confident that you'll be able to manage payments consistently throughout the loan term.

4. Credit Counseling and Debt Management Plans: Credit counseling is a service that can help you evaluate your financial situation and provide guidance on how to improve your financial health. Credit counselors may recommend a debt management plan (DMP) if they find that it's the most suitable option for your situation. A DMP involves negotiating with your creditors to lower your interest rates, waive fees, and create an affordable repayment plan.

You'll make a single monthly payment to the credit counseling agency, which will then distribute it among your creditors. Keep in mind that enrolling in a DMP may impact your credit score initially, but making consistent payments will improve it over time.

5. Debt Settlement: Debt settlement is the process of negotiating with your creditors to pay off your debt for less than what you owe. This option should be considered as a last resort because it can significantly impact your credit score. Debt settlement companies usually require you to stop making payments on your debts, directing those funds into a savings account instead. Once you have saved enough money, the debt settlement company will attempt to negotiate with creditors on your behalf.

Each debt consolidation option comes with its pros and cons. To choose the most suitable one for you, assess your financial situation carefully and consider factors such as your credit score, employment stability, and current interest rates.

Remember that while debt consolidation is an excellent tool for managing and reducing high-interest debts, it's not a cure-all solution. Adopting responsible financial habits – like creating and sticking to a budget, not spending more than you earn, and savings for emergencies – lies at the core of lasting financial freedom.

AVOIDING COMMON DEBT TRAPS

It is crucial to identify and avoid the common debt traps that can derail our progress. Below are the practical strategies, habits, and mindset shifts that will empower you to escape and prevent these financial pitfalls.

1. High-Interest Credit Cards: One of the most insidious debt traps is getting caught in a cycle of high-interest credit card debt. A simple swipe might seem harmless at first glance, but it can eventually snowball into mounting interests and a crippling debt burden.

Avoid this trap by prioritizing the elimination of high-interest debts. Prioritize payments on credit cards with the highest interest rates, and consider transferring your balance to a zero-percent interest or low-interest card if possible. Be disciplined in paying your balance in full every month and resist the urge to spend beyond your means.

2. Payday Loans: They might be tempting as an immediate solution for cash-flow problems, but payday loans are another common debt trap that can wreak havoc on your finances. With exorbitant interest rates and fees, these loans can quickly cycle out of control, leading to more borrowing or falling behind on other payments.

To avoid payday loans altogether, create an emergency fund comprising three to six months' worth of living expenses. This fund will serve as a safety net during those unexpected financial emergencies when you may have considered resorting to payday loans.

3. Overspending on a Home: Many people aspire to own a dream home and often fall into the trap of overspending on their property investment—taking a mortgage that's too large or buying a more expensive house than they can afford over time.

The key here is to be realistic about what you can truly afford and diligently search for a home that fits within your budget. If possible, aim for a mortgage payment that's no more than 25% of your monthly take-home pay, and don't forget to consider other expenses like insurance, taxes, and maintenance.

4. Co-signing Loans: Helping family or friends by co-signing a loan might feel like the right thing to do; however, you might be unknowingly stepping into a debt trap. Remember, when you co-sign a loan, you become legally obligated to pay if the borrower defaults.

To steer clear of this trap, never co-sign for someone who isn't financially responsible. If you feel compelled to help someone, consider offering monetary assistance without putting your own financial health at risk.

5. Failing to Budget: Lastly, the absence of a proper budget can also lead us into debt traps. Many individuals live paycheck to paycheck without realizing their day-to-day spending patterns are causing them to inch closer towards financial ruin.

Commit to creating a monthly budget that outlines your income and expenses. Ensure your expenses do not exceed your earnings and allocate some funds towards savings and debt repayment. Regularly review and adjust your budget as needed.

BOOK FOUR

PROTECTING YOUR CREDIT

INTRODUCTION

The fourth book in the CREDIT SECRETS BIBLE 5 in 1 series is all about protecting your credit. Ensure that your hard-earned credit score is safe from identity theft risks by learning to recognize potential threats as well as actively safeguarding your personal information. Familiarize yourself with security measures like regular monitoring, rebuilding after fraud instances, and effectively using Section 609 Letter templates for dispute resolution.

<h1 style="text-align:center">CHAPTER 10
IDENTITY THEFT PREVENTION</h1>

IDENTITY THEFT OCCURS WHEN SOMEONE GAINS UNAUTHORIZED ACCESS TO YOUR PERSONAL AND financial information and uses it for malicious purposes, such as opening accounts in your name or draining funds from your existing accounts. This can result from various sources – cybercriminals hacking into databases, phishing emails tricking you into submitting sensitive data, or even old-fashioned pickpockets swiping your wallet or purse.

Preventing identity theft starts with an understanding of how these thieves operate and staying vigilant in protecting your information. Let's delve into some critical measures you can take to ensure that your identity remains firmly within your control.

RECOGNIZING IDENTITY THEFT RISKS

Identity theft is a crime that occurs when someone illegally obtains your sensitive data and uses it to impersonate you for malicious purposes. One major identity theft risk comes from cyber criminals who target vulnerable individuals or systems to steal sensitive information. They may use banks, government agencies, healthcare providers, retail outlets, or even seemingly harmless email links to achieve this. These individuals are often well-versed in social engineering tactics, enabling them to tap into human emotions like fear or greed to make victims fall into their traps.

Phishing scams are a prevalent risk that entice victims to click on dangerous links or share private data through deceitful messages. The same goes for phone scams where criminals pose as someone they're not, such as tax officers, bank personnel, or even a friend in need of help, to gain your trust and pry personal details from you.

Data breaches are another significant threat to be aware of when recognizing identity theft risks. Poorly secured companies with access to your private information may suffer from a security breach that exposes data like usernames, passwords, addresses and financial information. Staying informed about the companies you share your details with and monitoring news alerts for reported breaches can safeguard against this risk.

PROTECTING PERSONAL INFORMATION

Your credit can make or break your financial life, and the key to maintaining impeccable credit lies in keeping your sensitive data safe. Here are various ways to protect your personal information and maintain control over your credit.

1. **Internet Safety Measures:** The internet is a fantastic resource for almost anything, but it also comes with its own set of dangers and potential security breaches when it comes to personal information. One of the essential steps in protecting your sensitive data is ensuring that your internet connection and devices are secure.

   - Use a reliable antivirus software and update it regularly.
   - Create strong, unique passwords for each of your online accounts.
   - Enable two-factor authentication whenever possible.
   - Be cautious while entering personal information on websites – ensure that they are secure by verifying the lock icon in the browser's address bar, or check if the web address begins with 'https://' (the 's' stands for secure).
   - Avoid using public Wi-Fi networks as much as possible; instead, opt for private VPN connections.

2. **Be Vigilant Against Phishing Scams:** A growing number of malicious emails and phone calls target unsuspecting individuals by posing as familiar companies or government organizations in an attempt to steal their personal information. These "phishing" scams can lead to identity theft and financial loss.

   - Never click on links or download attachments from unfamiliar sources in emails.
   - Verify the sender's information before responding; never trust email addresses blindly.
   - Avoid sharing personal information over phone calls from unknown sources – always verify an organization's contact details through official channels first.

3. **Keep Physical Documents Secure:** While much focus goes into securing digital information, it's necessary not to overlook the importance of keeping physical copies of your sensitive data safe.

   - Shred or destroy any documents containing personal information before discarding them.
   - Store essential documents, like identification and financial records, in a secured location like a lockbox or safe.
   - Opt for electronic billing and e-statements where possible to reduce the amount of sensitive information being delivered in paper form.

4. **Monitor Your Credit:** Regularly checking your credit report is crucial to ensure that your personal information hasn't been misused. Examine your credit reports for any inconsistencies, such as unfamiliar accounts or inaccurate personal information.

- Request a free annual credit report from each of the major credit reporting agencies (Equifax, Experian, and TransUnion).
- Consider signing up for a credit monitoring service; many provide notifications about significant changes to your credit report.

5. Restrict Unnecessary Access: In many instances, people inadvertently give out their personal information without considering the consequences. Be mindful of the places and situations where you share your data.

- Never provide your social security number unless it's genuinely essential.
- Limit the amount of information you share on social media – not everyone needs to know your date of birth or phone number.

6. React Quickly In Case Of Identity Theft: Despite taking all the necessary precautions, if you find yourself in a situation where your personal information has been compromised, timely action can help limit the damage.

- Report the incident to the relevant financial institutions.
- File a police report and keep a copy for your records.
- Put a fraud alert on your credit reports – this makes it harder for an identity thief to open new accounts using your details.

RESPONDING TO IDENTITY THEFT

As you turn the pages of the Credit Secrets Bible, you'll find a wealth of knowledge to help you prevent any damage to your financial reputation. However, even the most cautious individuals may find themselves as victims of identity theft. Knowing how to respond can save you time, money, and future heartache.

Imagine this scenario: You receive a call from your credit card company about an unusual purchase made on your account. Your heart sinks as you realize that it's not just an oversight on your part – someone is actively using your personal information for their gain. Below are the steps to take in response to identity theft.

1. Confirm the Fraud: The first step is to confirm that fraud has indeed occurred. Reach out to other accounts or financial institutions where you suspect your information may have been compromised and gather evidence in preparing for next steps.

2. Inform Affected Institutions: Upon confirmation of the fraudulent activity, immediately notify all affected financial institutions, be it banks or credit card companies, so they can take precautionary measures such as freezing the account or canceling the card.

3. Reset Your Passwords: Change passwords and PINs for bank accounts, email and social media platforms compromised by the identity theft. Use complex passwords with a mixture of uppercase and lowercase letters, numbers, and special characters.

4. Alert Credit Bureaus: Contact all three credit bureaus – Equifax, Experian, and TransUnion – and request them to place a fraud alert on your credit file. This alerts creditors that they should take additional steps in verifying your identity before extending credit in your name with businesses.

5. File a Police Report: File a police report by contacting your local law enforcement office or precinct and providing them with necessary details about the supposed theft incidents. The report can serve as useful documentation when communicating with creditors or disputing charges in the future.

6. Report the Crime to Government Agencies: Report identity theft to government agencies like Federal Trade Commission (FTC) or your country's equivalent. Doing so allows authorities to track and monitor trends in identity theft and proactively educate consumers on potential risks.

7. Document Everything: Keep detailed records of all correspondence with financial institutions, creditors, law enforcement, and any other agencies you have interacted with as a result of the theft situation. This documentation is crucial for future reference or legal purposes should the need arise.

8. Monitor Your Credit: Closely monitor your credit reports for any discrepancies or warning signs of further fraud. It is advised that you review your reports from all three bureaus at least once a year.

9. Credit Monitoring Services: Consider using a credit monitoring service that will keep a close eye on your credit report for any potential signs of fraudulent activity – typically for a monthly fee. These services will notify you of changes in your credit report, such as new accounts being opened or inquiries being made.

10. Check Your Insurance: Review your homeowner's insurance policy as some policies include coverage for identity theft protection or recovery costs. You could benefit from having financial support in taking necessary steps to remedy the damage caused by identity fraud.

Facing identity theft can feel like a daunting experience. Remember, while these steps may seem burdensome now, acting quickly and decisively will help you regain control of your credit score and financial life.

CHAPTER 11
CREDIT MONITORING AND SECURITY

IMPLEMENTING AN EFFECTIVE CREDIT MONITORING SYSTEM CAN HELP YOU STAY UP-TO-DATE WITH ANY changes in your credit report. It allows you to review any modifications in real-time and spot potential issues early on that may be detrimental to your credit standing.

Credit monitoring services track changes in your credit report by regularly evaluating the information provided by lenders, creditors, and public records. These services notify you when any essential updates are made to ensure that your financial position remains secure and transparent at all times.

BENEFITS OF CREDIT MONITORING

One of the primary advantages of credit monitoring is the ability to track your credit score and report continuously. It helps you identify any discrepancies or suspicious activities in your accounts that may affect your credit health adversely. Timely detection of such aberrations enables you to take immediate remedial measures and protect your credit from potential damage.

Credit monitoring equips you with vital information about your borrowing habits, which helps you recognize areas in which you can improve. A higher credit score means better opportunities for obtaining loans at lower interest rates, making life more comfortable and enabling you to save money on future transactions.

Another significant benefit of credit monitoring is safeguarding your identity. With incidents of identity theft on the rise, constant vigilance has become more critical than ever. By keeping an eye on your accounts and alerting you at the first sign of any suspicious activity, credit monitoring acts as your first line of defense against identity theft. If not nipped in the bud, identity theft can lead to severe financial consequences and take months or even years to rectify.

Having regular access to your credit score also helps you set and track realistic financial goals. Knowing how close or far away you are from achieving an excellent credit rating can serve as much-needed motivation, empowering you to strive harder by making smarter choices, like paying off debts promptly or taking on additional lines of credit prudently.

Another indirect benefit comes from improved financial literacy through being actively involved in monitoring your credit. Understanding what factors contribute positively or negatively to your credit score allows you to adapt your financial behavior. With greater control over your finances, you can pursue additional monetary opportunities confidently.

Furthermore, credit monitoring helps in catching inaccuracies in your credit reports before they hurt your credit score. Whether it's a simple clerical error or a report of a loan that you didn't take, such inconsistencies should be flagged and addressed as soon as possible to prevent long-term damage.

One more advantage of credit monitoring is easing the process of disputing errors in your credit report. This service aids in identifying inaccuracies and assists you in lodging disputes with the concerned credit bureaus conveniently. A corrected credit report can result in a much more accurate representation of your true financial standing, ensuring that you're not unfairly denied any well-deserved opportunities.

Finally, having an excellent credit score gives you the psychological benefit of peace of mind. Knowing that you're on the right track financially can significantly reduce stress and anxiety related to money matters, allowing for better focus on other important aspects of life.

TIPS FOR SECURING YOUR CREDIT

Securing your credit profile should be of the utmost importance, especially with the prevalence of identity theft and data breaches. Luckily, we have compiled a list of tips that will help you secure your credit- ensuring better financial stability.

1. Monitor Your Credit Reports: Begin by keeping a close eye on your credit reports. Know what information is maintained in those records, ensuring no fraudulent activity goes unnoticed. By law, you are entitled to one free credit report from each of the major reporting agencies (Equifax, Experian, and TransUnion) every year. Review your reports for any inaccuracies or suspicious activities.

2. Consider Using Credit Monitoring Services: Subscribe to a reliable and secure credit monitoring service if monitoring your reports on an annual basis doesn't suffice. These services can help you keep track of changes in your credit history by sending higher-frequency updates than the once-a-year free reports.

3. Safeguard Your Personal Information: Be meticulous when it comes to safeguarding your personal information. Shred sensitive documents before discarding them to avoid identity theft. Do not share critical data such as bank account numbers or social security numbers easily online or over the phone unless you are sure of the authenticity of the recipient.

4. Create Strong Passwords for Online Accounts: Ensure that you have strong passwords for all your online accounts related to banking or financial matters. Use a mix of uppercase and lowercase letters, number combinations, and symbols to make it difficult for hackers to access your accounts.

5. Be Watchful of Security Questions: When using security questions for password recovery purposes on your accounts, opt for ones that are difficult to guess and not evident from your public profiles. Utilize unique answers instead of common information that can be easily discovered.

6. Enable Two-Factor Authentication: Two-factor authentication (2FA) adds an extra layer of security to your online accounts by requiring access through multiple verification processes. Enable 2FA on all your accounts related to personal finances.

7. Avoid Public Wi-Fi Networks: Public Wi-Fi networks pose an increased risk of identity theft and hacking. Avoid using them to access important financial information or websites that require entering sensitive data.

8. Regularly Update Your Devices: Ensure you timely update your devices with the latest security patches and anti-virus software. These updates equip your devices with the latest capabilities to protect against cyber threats.

9. Set Up Alerts for Credit Card Transactions: Many banks offer an alert system to keep you updated on transactions carried out using your credit cards. Set up these alerts for any activity on your account to efficiently track fraudulent activities or unauthorized purchases.

10. Place a Credit Freeze on Your Reports: A credit freeze restricts access to your credit report, making it difficult for identity thieves to open fraudulent accounts under your name. However, it is essential to know that a credit freeze can delay or interfere with loan applications or other credit services that require access to your report. Use this option cautiously.

RECOVERING FROM CREDIT FRAUD

From the moment you discover you've fallen victim to credit fraud, you must act swiftly to regain control of your financial life. In this section, we will walk you through the process of recovering from credit fraud, repairing your credit score, and making sure you never face such a stressful ordeal again.

1. Immediate Action: The moment you realize that your credit identity has been compromised, embrace the urgency of the situation. Be swift in contacting the bank or credit card issuer and inform them about the fraudulent activity. This will allow them to freeze or cancel your card, preventing further transactions while investigations are underway.

2. Awakening Vigilance: Once your account is secure, compile an exhaustive report encompassing every unauthorized transaction to be shared with your bank or credit card issuer. Additionally, notify law enforcement agencies about the incidents by filing a report with your local police department.

3. Discover Strength in Unity: Contact all three major credit bureaus (Equifax, Experian, and TransUnion) to place a fraud alert on your credit reports. This proactive step not only protects you from additional fraudulent activities but also notifies potential creditors to exercise caution before approving new credit applications in your name.

4. Venturing Beyond Banking Institutions: Complete an Identity Theft Affidavit provided by the Federal Trade Commission (FTC) as an affirmation of your claim that someone has indeed used your personal information without consent. This document solidifies your claim and serves as essential evidence while resolving disputed charges with creditors.

5. Battle on Multiple Fronts: Unfortunately, identity theft can extend beyond banks and credit institutions. There have been numerous instances of tax fraud wherein delinquents file tax returns using stolen identities to claim the refund fraudulently. Report any such suspicions to the Internal Revenue Service (IRS) and your state's tax agency – consider applying for an Identity Protection PIN as a preventative measure.

6. Elevate Your Defenses: As part of your recovery process, invest in credit monitoring services that provide personalized alerts tailored to identify unusual activities in your accounts.

Empower yourself with the information collected by these companies, fortifying your financial fortress against any external breach or infiltration.

7. Embrace the Journey: A recovery from credit fraud is never an overnight endeavor; it takes time, patience, and perseverance. Make consistent efforts to review outstanding debts, resolve discrepancies, and take steps to build a healthier credit score – remember that taking responsibility means embracing progress.

8. Summon Resilience: As you slowly emerge victorious from your credit fraud ordeal, ensure that safeguards are in place to avoid such occurrences in the future. Invest in secure passwords, explore two-step verification options, and educate yourself about the ever-evolving world of credit card scams and identity theft.

CHAPTER 12
USING 609 LETTER TEMPLATES FOR CREDIT REPAIR

THE TERM "609" REFERS TO SECTION 609 OF THE FAIR CREDIT REPORTING ACT (FCRA), WHICH outlines vital information that consumers have the right to request from credit reporting agencies. A 609 Letter, therefore, is a written correspondence you send to credit bureaus to exercise your rights under this particular provision of FCRA. It focuses on the verification and validation of debt entries on your credit report.

The primary objective of a 609 Letter is to request proof of validation or dispute inaccuracies in your credit report. To ensure success with this approach, it's essential to familiarize yourself with some critical elements that every effective 609 Letter must-have:

1. Personal Information: Always include accurate personal details such as full name, Social Security Number, address, and date of birth in your 609 Letter. This information helps credit bureaus identify your record and respond accordingly.

2. Clear Intent: Express your intention to validate the debt entry or dispute the inaccuracies on your credit report explicitly. Be specific about which items require attention and pose relevant questions to seek clarification or dispute the information.

3. Request for Documentation: Invoke your rights under Section 609 of the FCRA and demand all documentation that can help you verify if the reported debt is accurate and belongs to you.

4. Proof of Response Timeline: Remember to include a statement that emphasizes the 30-day window within which the credit bureaus must respond, as mandated by FCRA.

5. Assertiveness with Courtesy: While it's essential to be assertive in your request, ensure that you maintain a polite tone throughout the letter. Avoid any language that may come across as aggressive or confrontational.

Once you've drafted your 609 Letter, make sure you send it via Certified Mail with a return receipt requested so that you can track its delivery and maintain evidence of correspondence.

Remember, though, that while a 609 Letter is undoubtedly an empowering tool for disputing inaccuracies, it may not guarantee instantaneous results. Credit repair is often a marathon, not a sprint, and patience will go a long way as you continue to strategize with other tactics mentioned in the Credit Secrets Bible.

WHEN TO USE A 609 LETTER

So when should you take advantage of this powerful tool? Here are some ideal scenarios:

1. Unverifiable Records: If you come across questionable items on your credit report that cannot be verified by you or the creditors themselves, it's time for a 609 Letter. By invoking your rights under Section 609, you can demand that the reporting agencies provide proof that these mysterious entries are indeed accurate and valid; if they fail to do so, they must remove them from your reports.

2. Outdated Negative Information: The FCRA mandates that most negative items be removed from your reports after seven years (bankruptcy being an exception at ten years). However, sometimes these items may linger past their expiration date. In such cases, use a 609 Letter to remind those pesky reporting agencies of their obligations and demand removal.

3. Identity Theft and Fraud: If you've been a victim of identity theft or fraud, a multitude of fraudulent activities could plague your report. In this scenario, a 609 Letter can help you unravel the web of inaccuracies and pave the way for a cleaner credit slate.

But remember, timing is critical. It's essential to have checked your credit reports thoroughly before taking any action. Ideally, a 609 Letter should be your go-to move when disputes with creditors have proved fruitless or when you need additional leverage to push them over the edge towards resolution.

CREATING AN EFFECTIVE 609 LETTER

Named after Section 609 of the Fair Credit Reporting Act (FCRA), this strategic document helps you exercise your legal rights in chasing a more accurate and fair credit report. By the end of this section, you'll become skilled in crafting a compelling 609 letter that demands attention.

1. Understand your rights: Before we reveal the secrets to crafting a powerful 609 letter, it's vital to understand your legal rights under the FCRA. Section 609 requires credit bureaus to provide consumers with accurate credit reports and disclose all information they have on file about them – including public records and personal identifiable data. By leveraging these rules, you can ensure that any negative information is adequately substantiated and accurately reported.

2. Obtain and analyze your credit reports: Start by obtaining copies of your credit reports from all three major bureaus – Equifax, Experian, and TransUnion. You're entitled to one free report per year from each bureau via AnnualCreditReport.com. Review your reports diligently, identifying any inaccuracies or incorrect negative items. This process forms the foundation for constructing an authoritative 609 letter.

3. Write a persuasive letter: With your list of dubious entries in hand, it's time to draft a compelling 609 letter. Begin with clarifying your intent – requesting verification of specific information under Sections 609 and 611 of the FCRA. Be concise yet encompassing while outlining each disputed item; provide necessary details like the creditor's name, account number, and specific reasons for your dispute.

4. Include relevant supporting documentation: To bolster your case, attach copies of any relevant documentation that supports your dispute. This may include bank statements, identity theft affidavits, or other financial records. Remember to only include photocopies, retaining the originals for your own files.

5. Request a response within the timeframe: According to the FCRA, credit bureaus must investigate your dispute within 30 days. Therefore, emphasize this deadline in your letter while politely asking for prompt action. Ensure you request a revised credit report and an update sent to any lenders who may have received incorrect information recently.

6. Proofread and send: Now that your letter is complete, proofread it thoroughly for errors and clarity. Send the letter via certified mail with a return receipt requested. This ensures you have proof of mailing and receipt by the credit bureau.

SENDING THE 609 LETTER

Sending a 609 letter is an important step in asserting your rights under the Fair Credit Reporting Act (FCRA) and addressing inaccuracies or outdated information on your credit report. The 609 letter allows you to request verification of debt from the credit bureaus and ensures that the debts they report are valid and belong to you.

Step 1: Obtain Your Credit Reports- Before sending a 609 letter, it's crucial to obtain your credit reports from all three major credit bureaus – Experian, Equifax, and TransUnion. You can request one free report per year from each bureau through AnnualCreditReport.com.

Step 2: Review Your Credit Reports- Carefully review each credit report for inaccuracies or outdated information. Make note of any negative items that you wish to dispute, such as incorrect account balances or falsely-reported late payments.

Step 3: Prepare Your 609 Letter- When crafting your 609 letter, be sure to include:

- Your full name, address, and Social Security number
- The account number(s) you're disputing
- A description of the disputed item(s)
- A statement that you're requesting validation of the debt under Section 609 of the FCRA
- A request for removal of unverified information
- Copies (not originals) of any supporting documents that prove your claim

Remember not to admit responsibility for any debts you're disputing; instead, ask the credit bureaus to validate that they have documentation proving these debts are legitimate and yours.

Step 4: Send Your Letter via Certified Mail- Sending your letter through certified mail with a return receipt is the best way to ensure that it reaches its destination and provides proof of delivery. This allows you to track your letter's progress and confirm its receipt by the credit bureaus.

Send your 609 letter to each of the three credit bureaus separately, as their verification processes and responses may vary. Their mailing addresses are:

Experian
 P.O. Box 4500
 Allen, TX 75013

Equifax Information Services LLC
P.O. Box 740256
Atlanta, GA 30374

TransUnion LLC
Consumer Dispute Center
P.O. Box 2000
Chester, PA 19016

Step 5: Wait for a Response- Under the FCRA, the credit bureaus have 30 days to investigate your dispute and provide a written response. During this time, they must contact the entity that provided the disputed information and request verification of the debt.

Step 6: Review the Credit Bureau's Findings- Once you receive their response, review the findings carefully. They should inform you if they were able to verify the disputed information or not. If they were unable to verify an item or failed to respond within the given time frame, they must remove it from your credit report.

Step 7: Follow Up If Necessary- If any of your disputes remain unresolved after receiving responses from the credit bureaus, consider sending a follow-up letter reiterating your request for investigation and removal of unverified items.

RESPONSES FROM CREDIT BUREAUS

As mandated by Section 609 of the Fair Credit Reporting Act (FCRA), credit bureaus are required to provide consumers with all pertinent information pertaining to their credit history and to verify any disputed information. The process starts when you send a detailed, yet succinct, 609 Letter to the applicable credit bureau(s), requesting the validation of one or more items featured on your report.

Upon receiving your letter, the bureau may respond in a few different ways:

1. Verification and removal of disputed items: In some cases, the credit bureau will promptly verify and subsequently remove the disputed item due to insufficient documentation or inability to prove its accuracy. This favorable resolution boosts your credit score and is an ideal outcome.

2. Confirmation without removal: Alternatively, the bureau may find adequate proof to support its initial claim and thereby uphold the contested item on your report. Should this occur, it is crucial that you carefully review any documents provided by the bureau to confirm their legitimacy before considering further action.

3. No response within 30 days: If you have not received any communication from the credit bureau after 30 days post-submission of your letter, this signifies their failure to respond within FCRA's stipulated time frame—a valuable oversight that can be leveraged to improve your credit score. By sending a follow-up letter citing their non-compliance with FCRA regulations, you could potentially expedite removal of negative items from your report.

4. Incomplete or unsatisfactory response: If the credit bureau's response is found to be lacking necessary information or fails to satisfy your demands, it is crucial that you clearly outline their inadequacies in a well-organized rebuttal letter. Subsequently, insist that they provide complete and accurate verification of the disputed information or promptly remove it from your report.

To ensure optimal results from a 609 Letter, it is essential that you exercise due diligence throughout the entire process. Maintain clear and concise communication with credit bureaus, track dates carefully, and dedicate yourself to comprehending the complexities of credit repair laws and regulations.

CHAPTER 13
SUCCESS STORIES AND CASE STUDIES

IN THIS CHAPTER, WE WILL DISCUSS TWO REMARKABLE SUCCESS STORIES AND CLOSELY EXAMINE TWO case studies to further understand the power of managing credit effectively. As we dive into these real-life experiences, you will see how individuals can rebuild their credit over time and achieve financial goals while dealing with various challenges.

JOURNEY FROM DEBT TO FINANCIAL FREEDOM

Jane was a single mother working two jobs to make ends meet. Her income was barely enough to cover her living expenses and the mounting debts from her divorce. No matter how hard she worked, it never seemed to be enough. Every month, her credit card balances grew larger, resulting in a lower credit score and limited access to affordable financing options.

As the stress increased, Jane became desperate for a solution. She stumbled upon "Credit Secrets Bible" while searching online one late-night. After reading the testimonials about the book's strategies, Jane decided to give it a try.

Within two weeks of employing its techniques, Jane noticed improvements in her credit score and general financial outlook. The comprehensive guide taught her how dispute inaccuracies on her credit report as well as negotiate better interest rates on existing loans. With newfound confidence, Jane began trimming excess spending from her budget and developing healthier financial habits.

The real turning point came when Jane discovered the concept of debt consolidation – combining multiple high-interest debts into a single loan with a lower interest rate and more manageable monthly payments. She applied for a debt consolidation loan through her local credit union and used it to pay off her overwhelming high-interest credit card balances.

Soon enough, Jane began seeing tangible results in her financial life: an increasing credit score, reduced overall interest payments on loans, and an improvement in cash flow each month. This improvement allowed her to make bigger payments on other debts and start saving for emergencies for the first time in years.

Today, Jane is free from the burden of high-interest debts and is on track to achieve her long-term financial goals, such as buying a house. Her journey to financial freedom started with the wisdom found within the pages of the "Credit Secrets Bible," paving the way to a brighter future for Jane and her family.

ELIMINATION OF A TAX LIEN AND START OF A NEW BUSINESS

David was a successful entrepreneur, but even he couldn't escape financial setbacks. When his business started declining, he had to file for bankruptcy. Unfortunately, this led to unpaid taxes and eventually resulted in a tax lien on his credit report—a dream-crushing blow for someone trying to rebuild their life.

Despite this setback, David didn't give up; he knew he had the skills and determination necessary to overcome these challenges. He searched for resources that could help him improve his credit score and found the "Credit Secrets Bible."

The book became David's go-to resource, revealing practical tips that helped him dispute errors in his credit report, remove outdated accounts, establish new lines of credit, and improve his credit's overall health.

With the guidance from the book, David managed to remove the tax lien from his credit report after negotiating with the IRS. The process involved paying off his delinquent taxes and demonstrating good faith that he could remain financially responsible moving forward.

Armed with this knowledge and a clean credit report, David started rebuilding his business. It began with securing low-interest loans—even after all he'd been through—and gradually expanded into ancillary markets. With each passing day, his entrepreneurial spirit drove him forward.

In just two years since discovering the "Credit Secrets Bible," David's once-struggling business is now thriving. Furthermore, he's reestablished himself as an entrepreneur all while maintaining solid financial habits that will keep him out of trouble in the years ahead.

These success stories showcase how individuals—facing seemingly insurmountable obstacles—chose not only to survive but also to flourish, with the help of the "Credit Secrets Bible." Jane and David's transformation journeys can serve as inspiration for all those dealing with financial trials. After all, if they can climb their way out of despair, so too can anyone who is plagued by mounting debt or crippled by a low credit score. The key lies in taking the first steps toward financial freedom and embracing the tools that can help get you there—beginning with the powerful knowledge hidden within this impactful book.

CASE STUDY 1: RECOVERING FROM BANKRUPTCY

Meet Mike, a 36-year-old small business owner who had to file for bankruptcy three years ago. He was devastated by the financial and emotional burden that the process brought upon him and his family. After the dust settled, Mike realized that he needed to start rebuilding his credit if he wanted to get back on his feet.

The first step he took was analyzing his credit report for errors and inaccuracies. He discovered several significant mistakes that were preventing him from raising his credit score as quickly as possible. He then worked diligently on disputing these errors by writing well-crafted letters to the three major credit bureaus. After some time, the credit bureaus acknowledged and corrected these errors.

In addition, Mike set about creating a budget and devised a plan aimed at improving his financial habits. He established payment reminders for all of his debt obligations and made it a point to pay bills on time. Furthermore, he reduced some of his expenses by cutting non-essential spending – thereby allowing him to allocate more income towards paying down debts.

Within a year of following this disciplined approach, Mike started noticing substantial improvements in his credit score. He was even able to secure reasonable lending terms for an auto loan. As time went on, Mike continued working on improving his credit health; in just three years, he managed to increase his credit score by over 150 points.

This case study reflects just one example of how someone can bounce back after undergoing financial hardships like bankruptcy. By leveraging the tips covered in this book, you too can begin repairing any damages on your credit report and work towards achieving your financial goals.

CASE STUDY 2: SETTING A COLLEGE GRADUATE UP FOR CREDIT SUCCESS

Linda recently graduated from college with student loan debt looming over her head. Like most recent graduates, she now faced the harsh realities of finding employment while managing her debt obligations. Linda realized that building a strong credit history was essential to her future successes and financial stability.

Linda began by tackling her student loan debt head-on. She contacted her loan servicer to discuss her repayment options, requesting an income-driven repayment plan that would ease the burden on her finances as she entered the workforce. This enabled her to make regular, on-time payments towards her debt.

Next, she meticulously budgeted her expenses to ensure she could allocate funds for saving and investing in her future. By living frugally and prioritizing essential purchases, Linda was able to set aside money in her savings account while gradually increasing contributions into a retirement account.

To further bolster her creditworthiness and enhance available credit, Linda applied for a low-limit, secured credit card. She understood the importance of using this card responsibly – making modest purchases and promptly paying off her balance each month. In doing so, she displayed good credit habits that positively influenced her credit report and score.

Linda also supplemented her income by taking on part-time freelance work, giving her flexibility in managing finances more effectively. In time, she managed to save for a down payment on a used vehicle, which required securing an auto loan with reasonable terms. Again, making timely payments on this loan provided Linda with additional positive marks on her credit report.

Through discipline and perseverance, Linda set herself up for long-term financial success by implementing the advice detailed in this book. Her journey serves as a model for young adults navigating the economic landscape after graduation.

CHAPTER 14
TIPS AND BEST PRACTICES

LEGAL CONSIDERATIONS AND LIMITATIONS

THIS SECTION DELVES INTO THE LAWS, REGULATIONS, AND RESTRICTIONS THAT GUIDE AND PROTECT both consumers and credit institutions, ensuring a fair and transparent financial ecosystem. To begin with, let's examine the Fair Credit Reporting Act (FCRA). Enacted in 1970, the FCRA safeguards consumers' rights by promoting accuracy, fairness, and privacy in credit reporting information. It also regulates how credit reporting agencies (CRAs) collect, disseminate, and maintain consumer data. Key provisions of the FCRA include:

1. Accurate reporting: CRAs are required to report accurate information about consumers' credit histories. Consumers have the right to dispute any inaccurate or incomplete information in their reports, and CRAs must investigate such disputes within 30 days.

2. Limited access: Only those with a "permissible purpose," such as lenders evaluating loan applications or employers assessing job applicants' financial responsibility levels, can access consumers' credit reports.

3. Outdated information removal: Most negative information, such as late payments or bankruptcy filings older than seven years (or ten years for bankruptcies), must be removed from credit reports.

The Equal Credit Opportunity Act (ECOA) is another significant law that prohibits discrimination in granting credit. Under ECOA regulations, lenders cannot deny credit based on race, religion, national origin, gender, marital status, age (assuming legal age), receipt of public assistance income sources or exercise of rights under the Consumer Credit Protection Act.

Additionally, the Fair Debt Collection Practices Act (FDCPA) protects consumers against abusive debt collection practices employed by third-party debt collectors. Some behaviors prohibited under the FDCPA include:

1. Harassment or abuse: Collectors cannot use obscene language or threats of violence while collecting a debt. Repeated or continuous phone calls to annoy or harass the debtor are also prohibited.

2. False or misleading representation: Debt collectors cannot use deceptive practices, such as disguising themselves as government officials, making false threats of lawsuits, or misrepresenting the amount owed.

3. Unfair practices: Collectors cannot impose fees or charges in addition to the actual debt amount unless specifically allowed by law. They are also forbidden from depositing post-dated checks prematurely.

Consumers should be aware of their state's statute of limitations for debt collection – the period in which a creditor can sue a debtor to collect on a defaulted loan. This duration varies across states and types of debts but is generally between three to ten years from the last payment or activity on the account. It is essential to note that even though the time frame has passed, unpaid debts could still negatively impact credit reports for up to seven years.

Lastly, individuals seeking professional credit repair assistance should check their respective state laws regarding credit repair organizations. The Credit Repair Organizations Act (CROA) is a federal law regulating credit repair companies, prohibiting them from deceptive marketing practices and charging upfront fees before rendering their services.

ALTERNATIVE CREDIT REPAIR STRATEGIES

A low credit score can lead to higher interest rates on loans, difficulty in obtaining mortgages, and even hindrance in securing job offers. For those struggling with a less-than-stellar credit score, the journey to repair it may seem daunting; however, take heart in knowing that there are alternative credit repair strategies that can vastly improve your situation.

1. Debt Validation: One unconventional yet highly effective method is debt validation. This involves questioning the legality of the debt and requesting proof from the collection agency or creditor claiming you owe them money. If they cannot provide sufficient documentation verifying the debt, you may dispute it. This strategy not only gives you leverage in negotiating better terms but also could lead to the removal of negative items from your credit report.

2. Goodwill Letters: Sometimes, all it takes to improve your credit score is a goodwill letter. If you have a generally good payment history with an isolated missed or late payment, writing a letter to your creditor explaining the circumstances surrounding your hardship and asking them to remove the penalty could work wonders. Emphasize that such instances are rare and express your commitment to maintaining a stellar payment history.

3. Debt Settlement Negotiations: Debt settlement negotiations involve offering a lump sum amount to creditors or collectors, asking them in return to forgive a percentage of the remaining outstanding balance. This may help you avoid paying exorbitant fees or suffering legal consequences resulting from non-payment. While this method can save you money upfront, it's crucial to note that debt settlements can have lasting negative effects on your credit report.

4. Piggybacking Credit: Another practical option is piggybacking on someone else's excellent credit (with their permission). By becoming an authorized user on somebody else's credit card account – usually a responsible family member or close friend – you take advantage of their positive credit history to improve your own financial situation.

5. Credit-builder Loans: Credit-builder loans are a unique lending arrangement, specifically designed to help people build or rebuild their credit. The loan funds are held in a savings account and disbursed only upon complete repayment of the loan. With each payment made on time, your lender will report your positive payment history to credit bureaus, thus boosting your credit score.

6. Personal Tradelines: Adding personal tradelines (credit accounts) to your credit report offers another avenue for repairing bad credit. By opening new accounts and maintaining a timely payment history and low balances, you'll present a more favorable image to prospective lenders and demonstrate your ability to manage multiple lines of credit.

7. Secured Credit Cards: Secured credit cards are another powerful means of demonstrating responsible financial behavior. These cards require a security deposit that also serves as your line of credit, minimizing the risk for the lender while providing an opportunity for you to showcase good habits concerning credit card usage.

RESOURCES AND TEMPLATES

Here are various resources and templates that will assist you in improving your credit score, managing your debts, and making well-informed financial decisions. These tools are designed to help you navigate the complex world of credit with ease, giving you a better understanding of your credit history and how to repair it.

1. Credit Report Templates: One of the most important things you can do to improve your credit score is to regularly review your credit reports from the three major credit bureaus: Equifax, Experian, and TransUnion. To simplify this process, there are credit report templates available online that provide a user-friendly way to analyze your reports. These templates allow you to input all relevant information from each report in an organized manner so that you can easily identify any discrepancies or inaccuracies that may be affecting your credit score.

2. Dispute Letter Templates: If you find errors on your credit reports or inaccurate information provided by creditors, it is crucial to address these issues immediately. Various dispute letter templates can be found online to help you write a strong, professional letter to the appropriate party. These templates often include placeholders for important details such as disputing parties' contact information, the specific error found on the credit report, and any supporting documentation that may be included.

3. Budgeting Templates: Creating a comprehensive budget is an essential part of managing your finances and staying on top of debt repayments. Several budgeting spreadsheet templates exist online that can be customized to fit your unique financial situation. These tools provide an organized format for tracking your income and expenses and can help identify spending habits that may be hindering your ability to improve your credit score.

4. Debt Payoff Planning Tools: Paying off outstanding debts is key when working on improving your credit score; however, it can be challenging knowing which debt to tackle first or how much extra to allocate towards each debt. Debt payoff planning tools, such as debt snowball and debt avalanche calculators, allow you to input your debts' details, including balances and interest rates, to create a customized plan for paying off your debts. This will enable you to see the potential savings in interest and the overall time it will take you to become debt-free.

5. Credit Monitoring Services: Keeping track of changes to your credit score is essential when working on improving it. Credit monitoring services provide a convenient way to monitor your credit reports' progress from all three major credit bureaus and alert you when significant changes occur. Many services are available today, some at no cost or low-cost subscription models.

6. Educational Resources: A wealth of educational resources is available to assist in understanding credit scores, credit reports, and financial management better. These resources often include articles, guides, videos, and even online courses that cover credit repair strategies, budgeting skills, and more in-depth topics like understanding mortgages or navigating bankruptcy.

BOOK FIVE

LONG-TERM FINANCIAL PLANNING

INTRODUCTION

Concluding the CREDIT SECRETS BIBLE 5 in 1 series, this last book arms you with knowledge on long-term financial planning. Understand the importance of saving, investing, and retirement planning as keys to building wealth. Gain valuable insights into setting financial milestones and realizing your goals for financial independence. Finally, reflect on key credit strategies learned throughout the series and create a personalized credit action plan for continued success in your financial journey.

CHAPTER 15
SAVING AND INVESTING FOR THE FUTURE

THE IMPORTANCE OF SAVING

WHY SAVE? WITHOUT A DOUBT, THE KEY TO FINANCIAL SUCCESS IS HAVING A SOLID SAVINGS PLAN IN place. Aside from providing you with financial security, it instills a sense of discipline and responsibility. Moreover, saving money can help you attain your goals and weather life's inevitable financial storms.

One of the primary reasons for saving is setting yourself up for a comfortable retirement. Once you have retired, your stable income will cease or significantly reduce, and so it is crucial to have resources to fall back on during this time. Adequate savings will provide you with financial independence in your golden years, allowing you to enjoy life without stressing over monetary matters.

Another significant reason to prioritize saving is fulfilling long-term goals like purchasing a home or embarking on higher education. These milestones often require substantial funding that can be challenging to assemble at once. Developing healthy saving habits allows you to reach these objectives with ease in due course.

Saving also offers critical protection against unforeseen circumstances. Life is unpredictable, and emergencies such as accidents or losing your job can happen without warning. Having a designated emergency fund ensures that you do not plunge into debt or struggle with paying bills during these trying times.

By instilling good saving habits early on, you raise your chances of maintaining stellar credit scores. Consistently paying off debts and being financially stable reflects positively on your credit report. Consequently, when seeking loans, credit card approvals or signing leases in the future, robust credit scores and healthy finances can work wonders.

So how exactly can one cultivate a sustainable savings plan? The following tips offer an excellent place to start:

1. Budgeting: A cornerstone of a successful savings strategy is having a well-defined budget.

A budget allows you to track your income, expenses, and savings. It provides guidelines to prevent overspending and a clear portrait of your financial status.

2. Set realistic goals: When forming your saving plan, establish short-term and long-term goals. These provide direction and motivation for consistent saving.

3. Automate savings: Set up standing orders or direct transfers from your income account right into your savings account each month. Automatic saving eliminates the temptation of over-spending before committing to your savings allocation.

4. Reduce debt: Pay off existing debts as soon as possible to avoid mounting interest payments that can significantly impact your ability to save in the long run.

INVESTMENT BASICS

Right from the start, it's crucial to recognize that investing is different from saving. Investing involves putting your money to work for you by purchasing assets or securities that hold the potential to increase in value over time. Saving, on the other hand, refers to simply setting aside money in a conservative manner, such as a savings account or CD, with minimal risk and minimal returns.

A well-rounded investment portfolio encompasses several asset classes. The term 'asset class' refers to a group of similar investments with related characteristics. The three primary asset classes are:

1. Equities (stocks): These represent ownership in a company and give investors the right to share in the company's profits through dividends or capital appreciation.

2. Fixed income (bonds): These are loans made by investors to borrowers, typically governments or companies, that pay regular interest payments.

3. Cash equivalents (money market instruments): These short-term investments provide liquidity and minimal risk, including Treasury bills and certificates of deposit.

Each asset class has different levels of risk and return potential. Understanding their unique characteristics becomes vital when building your investment portfolio.

One of the key concepts in investing is diversification – spreading your investments across various asset classes to minimize overall risk. Diversification can help protect your portfolio from significant losses since market fluctuations impact each asset class differently.

Before making any investment decisions, it's essential to assess your risk tolerance. This term considers the degree of uncertainty you're willing to endure when it comes to your investments' value fluctuating over time.

Investors with low-risk tolerance are more comfortable with conservative investments like cash equivalents or bonds. Those with high-risk tolerance might prefer equities or alternative investments that offer potentially higher returns.

Every investor's journey is unique, and establishing clear goals can help you navigate the path to success. Consider your financial objectives, whether it be retirement planning, education funding, or wealth accumulation. Mapping out these targets on a timeline will enable you to make informed investment decisions.

Your investment time horizon is the period you expect to hold onto your investments before needing access to your funds. Longer time horizons typically allow investors to endure periods of market uncertainty since they have more time for their portfolios to recover.

Assembling your investment portfolio often involves selecting a mix of asset classes that aligns with your goals, risk tolerance, and time horizon. This process, called asset allocation, can help balance potential returns against inherent risk, paving the way for more stable growth over time.

Once you've established a suitable asset allocation strategy, it's time to consider specific investment vehicles like individual stocks or bonds, mutual funds, exchange-traded funds (ETFs), index funds, and more. Each vehicle has its benefits and drawbacks – it's essential to weigh these factors alongside performance track records and fees before making decisions.

Reviewing your investment performance periodically is crucial in maintaining your desired asset allocation and adjusting it as necessary in response to market conditions or changes in your financial objectives.

RETIREMENT PLANNING

Retirement planning is a crucial aspect of building a financially secure future. It allows you to create an income that supports your lifestyle when you no longer work, and it ensures that your lifelong financial goals are achieved. By implementing thoughtful retirement planning strategies at an early stage, you can secure your financial future and enjoy the fruits of your labor.

Let's explore the areas of retirement planning that you need to focus on to ensure the financial stability you deserve in your golden years.

1. Estimating Retirement Expenses: To begin, it's essential to have an idea of how your expenses will change once you retire. While some costs are expected to lessen, such as commuting and work-related expenses, others may increase, such as healthcare and leisure activities. Therefore, it's crucial to assess all potential expenses and adjust for inflation to achieve an accurate estimate of retirement living costs.

2. Identifying Income Sources: The next step is to identify potential sources of income during retirement. These may include Social Security benefits, employer-sponsored retirement plans (like a 401(k), IRA, or a pension), investments, savings accounts, and any other sources of passive income like rental property. Assessing these income streams helps you determine any funding gaps and adjust your planning strategies accordingly.

3. Creating a Savings Plan: After considering your estimated expenses and potential income streams, develop a savings plan if necessary—this plan should include regular contributions to various investment vehicles tailored specifically for your needs and objectives. The sooner you start saving for retirement, the more time your money has to grow through compound interest.

4. Diversification of Investments: When investing for retirement, it's essential to have a diverse portfolio spread across different asset classes like stocks, bonds, or real estate. Market fluctuations can impact different investments in varying ways; therefore, having a well-diversified portfolio may help minimize risks and ensure consistent returns over time. Seeking the assistance of a financial advisor can help tailor an investment strategy based on your financial goals and risk tolerance.

5. Maximizing Tax Advantages: Retirement accounts often offer tax advantages, which can significantly increase your retirement savings' growth potential. It's essential to optimize your contributions to tax-deferred accounts like 401(k)s and traditional IRAs to minimize tax liability at the present, allowing your money to grow faster before being taxed upon withdrawal.

6. Planning for Healthcare Expenses: Healthcare expenses are among the most significant financial burdens during retirement, especially as people live longer and healthcare costs continue to rise. Planning for these expenses early is crucial. Long-term care insurance policies or annuities with long-term care riders can alleviate the potential burden of significant healthcare costs, providing financial peace of mind.

7. Estate Planning: Estate planning plays a vital role in ensuring that your assets are distributed according to your wishes after you pass away. Proper estate planning also helps minimize potential estate taxes and eases the execution process for your loved ones.

CHAPTER 16
ACHIEVING FINANCIAL GOALS

FINANCIAL MILESTONES ARE LIKE CHECKPOINTS ON A ROADMAP TO YOUR ULTIMATE FINANCIAL GOALS. They keep you motivated, create a sense of achievement, and measure your progress. The following steps will help you establish and achieve significant milestones in your financial journey.

1. Define Your Financial Goals: Start by listing all your short-term, medium-term, and long-term financial objectives. Short-term goals might involve paying off credit card debt or establishing an emergency fund. Medium-term goals could include buying a home or funding a child's education. Long-term goals may involve saving for retirement or leaving a legacy for your family.

2. Prioritize Your Goals: Arrange your financial goals in order of importance to focus resources effectively on those most crucial to your overall success. This prioritization enables you to allocate funds and energy where they have the most impact on your financial life.

3. Set SMART Milestones: Transform each financial goal into a milestone using the SMART criteria:

- *Specific:* Define what must be accomplished in clear terms.
- *Measurable:* Determine how much progress can be tracked.
- *Achievable:* Ensure that the goal is realistic yet challenging.
- *Relevant:* Make sure it's meaningful to your overall objectives.
- *Time-bound:* Attach deadlines for achieving each milestone.

For example, instead of vaguely aiming to "pay off credit card debt," set a SMART milestone like, "Pay $10,000 in credit card debt within 18 months."

4. Create Action Plans: Develop coordinated strategies for reaching each milestone through budgeting adjustments, debt management plans, and investment opportunities presented in this book.

5. Monitor Progress: Faithfully track advancement toward each milestone through regular check-ins and evaluations. As you reach key checkpoints, recognize and celebrate these accomplishments, motivating yourself to continue.

6. Stay Flexible: Circumstances can change, so be prepared to revise your milestones as needed. Just as roadmaps might have detours or unexpected roadblocks, be open to adapting your plans without losing sight of your ultimate financial objectives.

Committing to these financial milestones will transform vague aspirations into concrete goals. With a clear roadmap to follow, you'll find success much easier to attain. Armed with the knowledge and strategies presented in this book, you can now set forth on your journey to financial freedom and security.

TRACKING PROGRESS

Achieving your financial goals requires constant monitoring, discipline, and sound decision-making. Here are various strategies to help you stay on top of your financial milestones and make adjustments as needed.

1. Set SMART Goals: The first step towards tracking your financial progress is setting Specific, Measurable, Achievable, Relevant, and Time-bound (SMART) goals. These goals will serve as your roadmap and provide a sense of direction to achieve financial milestones.

2. Keep a Budget: Maintaining a budget is a vital instrument for tracking the progress of your financial milestones. It involves categorizing your income and expenses into different accounts, thereby helping you identify spending patterns. This knowledge enables you to make wise decisions in allocating funds towards the achievement of your financial goals.

3. Use Financial Software or Tools: There are numerous financial software and apps available in the market that can help you track your progress efficiently. Some popular applications include Mint, Quicken, and You Need A Budget (YNAB). These applications automatically sync with your bank accounts and other financial institutions to provide real-time updates on your finances.

4. Review Your Progress Regularly: Schedule routine check-ins with yourself to review your progress towards achieving your financial milestones. This could be daily, weekly, or monthly – depending on personal preference or the nature of specific financial goals. Regular reviews will help you monitor trends in spending habits and make better decisions moving forward.

5. Monitor Your Credit Score: A healthy credit score can unlock numerous opportunities for improving one's financial situation. Consequently, it becomes essential to take proactive steps in monitoring and improving your credit score. Use free services like Credit Karma or annualcreditreport.com to review credit reports periodically and identify errors or discrepancies that can impact the score negatively.

6. Avoid Lifestyle Inflation: As your income increases, it's tempting to indulge in lavish lifestyles and overspending. However, this can severely impact your financial goals and hinder the progress of your milestones. To avoid lifestyle inflation, be mindful of unnecessary expenses and focus on saving money rather than raising expenditure levels.

7. Leverage Expertise: Hiring a financial planner or advisor can assist you in staying focused on achieving your financial milestones. The expertise of these professionals will make it easier for you to manage your financial situation actively.

8. Celebrate Small Victories: Acknowledge and celebrate the small victories as you work towards achieving your financial milestones. This will keep you motivated and focused on making continuous progress.

9. Re-evaluate and Adjust When Necessary: As life changes, so might your financial goals or the progress towards your milestones. It is crucial to re-evaluate and adjust your strategies when necessary, ensuring they align with current circumstances and priorities.

ADJUSTING YOUR FINANCIAL PLAN

The first key element in adjusting your financial plan is to recognize when changes in your life necessitate a review of your financial blueprint. These could be major events such as getting married or divorced, having a child, or starting a new business. Alternatively, they could be minor changes in circumstances such as switching jobs or receiving a promotion. Regardless of their scale, these life transitions may require you to adapt your financial plans to maintain focus on achieving your desired goals.

Once you have identified the need for change, reassessing your budget is crucial. Your budget may have suited you well in the past, but with new expenses or streams of income from life changes, it is essential that you modify it accordingly. Revise your budget by categorizing your income and expenses in relation to your updated priorities, ensuring that every dollar spent is serving a purpose that aligns with your current financial goals.

As part of adjusting your budget and spending habits, it's vital to be aware of the impact of inflation on your money's value. Over time, inflation can significantly reduce the purchasing power of your finances. In light of this realization, it becomes increasingly important to consider investment opportunities that can help mitigate inflation's adverse effects and maintain growth in line with your future expectations.

Alongside re-evaluating your budget and investment strategies to suit new circumstances, reassessing your savings plan is equally crucial. As our lives evolve over time, so do our long-term objectives for living expenses and emergency funds reserve. Take the opportunity to review your savings mechanisms, ensuring they are still relevant and capable of realizing your future aspirations.

Devising a contingency plan is another crucial step in adjusting your financial plan. Life is laden with unforeseen events that may impact your finances. Having a fallback strategy, such as an emergency fund or insurance policies, safeguards you against these uncertainties and lessens the risk of financial setbacks derailing your path to success.

Lastly, do not forget the importance of revisiting your credit situation as part of adjusting your financial plan. As life changes bring about new financial commitments, understanding how these transformations will impact your credit standing becomes increasingly vital. Reviewing your credit report regularly, ensuring information accuracy and addressing discrepancies should be an integral component of your ongoing financial management.

CHAPTER 17
FINANCIAL FREEDOM AND WEALTH BUILDING

BUILDING WEALTH OVER TIME

THE NOTION THAT WEALTH IS ACQUIRED OVERNIGHT IS A MISCONCEPTION; BUILDING WEALTH TAKES time, patience, and persistence. While it's important to address your credit issues to create a foundation for such growth, building wealth involves leveraging credit to generate assets that drive greater returns. Here are three key principles for accumulating wealth over time:

1. Save consistently: Every successful wealth-building strategy starts with saving money consistently. Set aside a portion of each paycheck in an interest-bearing account, such as a high-yield savings account or a certificate of deposit (CD). The miracle of compound interest will cause your savings to grow exponentially as you continue to save.

2. Invest wisely: As your savings grow, layer in investments that provide higher returns than traditional savings accounts – such as stocks, mutual funds, or real estate. Diversify your portfolio with a mix of long-term and short-term investments to minimize risk and enhance overall performance.

3. Utilize credit effectively: Building good credit requires proper management of your finances – including timely bill payments and maintaining low balances on revolving accounts like credit cards. Use your positive credit history to procure reasonable financing rates on loans for major purchases like homes or cars - these opportunities can dramatically impact one's capacity for wealth building.

STRATEGIES FOR FINANCIAL INDEPENDENCE

Financial independence means having enough income-generating assets to cover your living expenses without relying on active employment or other forms of intervention. Achieving this goal necessitates thoughtful planning and consistent execution. Here are three strategies for attaining financial independence:

1. Reduce debt: Start by paying off high-interest debt such as credit cards or personal loans.

The faster you eliminate these debts, the sooner you can allocate those monthly payments toward savings and investments. Prioritize your debts based on interest rates, starting with the highest rate first for maximum impact.

2. Establish multiple income streams: Relying on a single source of income limits your potential for financial independence. Aim to create multiple streams of revenue - be it through investment, side hustles, or passive-income-generating ventures – to diversify one's financial outlook.

3. Monitor and adapt: As life changes - from marriage and children to health issues and retirement - so too do your financial needs. Periodically review and adjust your wealth-building strategies to accommodate these evolutions. Stay informed about financial trends and market conditions that may impact the performance of your assets.

LEAVING A LEGACY

The journey toward financial freedom doesn't end when you attain wealth; it also involves preserving that wealth for future generations through legacy planning.

1. Build assets that last: Long-term assets such as real estate or stocks can prove valuable inheritances for your loved ones while continuously driving growth during your lifetime.

2. Estate planning: Draft essential estate-planning documents such as a will or trust specifying how your property should be distributed upon your demise. Seek legal counsel to ensure compliance with prevailing inheritance laws and minimize tax exposure.

3. Instill financial literacy: Encourage those in line to inherit your wealth to adopt sound financial habits and educate them on responsible investing, managing debt, and saving money effectively. This knowledge sharing reinforces the sustainability of one's legacy for generations to come.

The pursuit of financial freedom is a multifaceted process, intrinsically linked with credit management, long-term wealth accumulation, frugality, and astute investment strategies. By leveraging these principles in tandem with those detailed in previous chapters of this book, readers can inch closer to building lifelong wealth and a lasting financial legacy. Perseverance on this path toward financial freedom will set the stage for a prosperous future and the opportunity to leave a meaningful imprint on generations yet to come.

CONCLUSION

As we come to the end of *"CREDIT SECRETS BIBLE 5 in 1,"* it is essential to recap the vital credit strategies we have covered and discuss how you can put your personalized credit action plan into action. Financial freedom and wealth building are at your fingertips, and by continuing your financial journey, you will see significant results in no time.

RECAP OF KEY CREDIT STRATEGIES

Throughout this book, we have covered various credit strategies that can help you achieve financial freedom and embark on a successful wealth-building journey. Some of the crucial credit strategies discussed include:

1. Understanding your credit score: Knowing the various components of your credit score is essential for taking control of your financial health.

2. Building positive credit history: Establishing good credit habits can improve your score, making it easier to secure favorable loan terms.

3. Removing negative items and errors from your report: Eliminating inaccuracies can result in improved credit scores.

4. Reducing outstanding debt: Less debt equals a better debt-to-income ratio which may lead to lower interest rates.

5. Optimizing utilization rates: Maintaining a low credit utilization rate reflects responsible borrowing habits and positively affects your rating.

6. Smart use of secured/unsecured cards and loans: Leveraging various types of credit products helps diversify your portfolio and demonstrate your ability to handle multiple financial responsibilities.

CREATING YOUR PERSONALIZED CREDIT ACTION PLAN

Now that we have revisited the key strategies in this book, it's time to create a personalized plan that caters specifically to your needs and aspirations:

1. Assess your current situation: Begin by examining your financial state and identifying any obstacles hindering progress toward financial freedom.

2. Set realistic goals: Create targeted milestones reflecting the desired improvements in your credit ranking and overall finances.

3. Prioritize actions: Determine which steps should be taken first, such as paying off debt or disputing inaccurate items, based on your unique circumstances.

4. Develop a budget and savings plan: Allocate funds to your credit improvement strategies while setting money aside for emergency costs, investments, and wealth-building opportunities.

5. Monitor your progress: Regularly review your credit reports and scores to track improvements and ensure no new errors or inconsistencies arise.

Implementing these action items will help you achieve a brighter financial future by providing a clear roadmap tailored to you.

CONTINUING YOUR FINANCIAL JOURNEY

Financial freedom is not a one-time accomplishment, but a lifelong journey that requires dedication and discipline. As you move forward, be sure to:

1. Stay informed about new credit strategies that could further enhance your progress.

2. Continuously educate yourself on financial management, investment opportunities, and wealth-building techniques.

3. Make adjustments to your personalized credit action plan as necessary, depending on shifting goals or circumstances.

4. Network with others interested in building wealth and credit mastery; you might learn from their experiences or share valuable insights from your journey.

5. Stay positive and maintain good financial habits - setbacks may happen, but perseverance is key to long-term success.

Remember that patience, determination, and commitment are essential factors in this process; stay focused on your goals and keep striving for improvement. You have already taken the first steps by reading this book; now it's time to put what you've learned into action.

Thank you for sharing this journey with us and best of luck in attaining financial success!

Made in the USA
Las Vegas, NV
11 June 2024